Scotland
Edited by Michelle Afford

To Grandma

Love from Ruairidh

 Young**Writers**

First published in Great Britain in 2008 by:
Young Writers
Remus House
Coltsfoot Drive
Peterborough
PE2 9JX
Telephone: 01733 890066
Website: www.youngwriters.co.uk

SB ISBN 978-1 84431 482 9

Foreword

Young Writers was established in 1991 and has been passionately devoted to the promotion of reading and writing in children and young adults ever since. The quest continues today. Young Writers remains as committed to the nurturing of poetic and literary talent as ever.

This year's Young Writers competition has proven as vibrant and dynamic as ever and we are delighted to present a showcase of the best poetry from across the UK and in some cases overseas. Each poem has been selected from a wealth of *Little Laureates* entries before ultimately being published in this, our sixteenth primary school poetry series.

Once again, we have been supremely impressed by the overall quality of the entries we have received. The imagination, energy and creativity which has gone into each young writer's entry made choosing the poems a challenging and often difficult but ultimately hugely rewarding task - the general high standard of the work submitted ensured this opportunity to bring their poetry to a larger appreciative audience.

We sincerely hope you are pleased with this final collection and that you will enjoy *Little Laureates Scotland* for many years to come.

Contents

Drymen Primary School, Glasgow

Gregor Cooper (10)	16
Jake Marshall (10)	17
James Findlay (10)	17
Annabelle Ferguson (10)	18
Kirsten McCabe (10)	19
Jan Duncan (10)	20
Jamie Hall (9)	21
Josh Degg (9)	22
David Johnstone (10)	23
Cameron O'Donnell	24
Lewis Strachan (10)	25
Zoë Glen (10)	26
Ruth Hurley (9)	27
Aimee Bourbousson (10)	28
Robyn Gemmell	29
Louise Wright	30

Flora Stevenson Primary School, Edinburgh

Max Carter (7)	30
Sophia Madden (10)	31
Harriet Johnston (9)	31
Arran Mackintosh (7)	32
David McFarlan (11)	33
Emma Clouston (10)	33
Anna McLuckie (11)	34
Max Law (10)	34
Lee Hunter (11)	35
Freya Ruuskanen (7)	35
Connor Sinclair (11)	36

Foulford Primary School, Cowdenbeath

Connor McArthur (11)	36
Pavinder Singh	36
Conor Crichton (11)	37
Nicole Menzies	38
Dylan Stanton	38
Katie Wilson	38
Patrick Adamson (11)	39
Cara Scott	39
Amy Machray	39

Shaun Hunter (11)	40
Lewis Ratcliffe (10)	41
Louise	41
Reece Sealey	42
Nicole Wilkie (11)	42
Siobhan Maxwell	43

John Paul II Primary School, Glasgow

Chiara Quadrelli (10)	43
Caitlyn Ward (10)	44
Laura Houston (10)	44
Reagan Petrie (7)	44
Yasmin Shariff (10)	45
Shauna McAuley (9)	45
Megan McGregor (8)	45
Thesia Kamba Banza (11)	46
Aeron Birney (11)	46
Anthony McKinnon (11)	47
Kimberly Houghton (10)	47
Andrew Duffin (7)	48
Jay Kelly (10)	48
Jamie-Leigh Walker (10)	49
Reece Montague (10)	49
Megan Keenan (10)	50
Nathan Flanagan (10)	50
Michael Mutondoro (10)	50
Jamie Downie (11)	51
Rebekah Weston (10)	51
Rebecca Morton (10)	51
Andrew Scott (10)	52
Shannon McNulty (9)	52
Sean O'Neill (10)	53
Lauryn Coyle (8)	53
Jordyn Smith (11)	54
Laura Donnelly (8)	54
Morgan McCrimmon (9)	55
David Mundemba (8)	55
Monique Petrie (10)	56
Jody Taggart (10)	56
Scott Ramsay (7)	56
Christopher O'Donnell (10)	57

Megan Hardie (8)   57
Chelsea-Lee Moody (7)   57
Alex Carson (8)   58
Daniel Drummond (9)   58
Darcy McBride (9)   59
Dylan Griffin (9)   59
Dylan McAuley (10)   60
Charles Ball (9)   60
Abbie Morton (8)   60
Nicole Boag (9)   61
Caitlyn Tervit (8)   61
David McKenna (11)   61
Rachel Birney (9)   62
Lauren Donaghue (11)   62
Marcus Richford (10)   62
Meghan Miller (9)   63
Stephen Johnston (11)   63
Sean Laverty (9)   64
Lauren Kelly (10)   64

Knightswood Primary School, Glasgow
Scott Robertson (10)   64
Millar Hendry (10)   65
Amy Wilson (10)   65
Luke McGunnigle (10)   65
Amy Hopkins (7)   66
Lauren Doran (6)   66
Kara Patrick (7)   66
Josh Lawson   67
Ryan Gardner (7)   67
Leah McGunnigle (6)   67
Megan Tolland (7)   68
Courtney Johnston (7)   68
Russell McGill (7)   68
Megan Houghton (7)   69
Jade Doyle (6)   69
Michael Fitzpatrick (5)   69
Connor Doogan   70
Lauren Patrick (10)   70
Emma Quinn   70
Lesley Coia (10)   71

Lewis Harrison (10)	71
Leena Gurung (10)	71
Chantel Fraser (11)	72
Annalise Gillan	72
Paul Cairns	73
Sean Miller (10)	73

Langbank Primary School, Langbank

Kyle Rodger (8)	73
Jennifer Hemphill (11)	74
Ross Tyre (8)	74
Gavin Hemphill (8)	75
Eve Lapping (9)	75

Our Holy Redeemer's Primary School, Clydebank

Jason Gallacher (9)	75
Dario Cocozza (9)	76
Sarah Brown (9)	76
Morgan Bell (9)	76
Ross Ferrier (9)	77
Frankie Burns (9)	77
Courtney Gallagher (9)	77
Stephen Cullen (9)	78
Darren Dolan (9)	78
Anthony Smith (9)	78
Aaron Keenan (9)	79
Johanna Doyle (9)	79
Shannon Davidson (9)	80
Shelby McGuiness (9)	80

Overton Primary School, Greenock

Luke Stewart (9)	80
Cheyenne Adamson (10)	81
James Barclay (10)	81
Kristy McGunnigle (8)	81
Gemma Ferguson (9)	82
Aidan Conway (10)	82
Erin Edwards (8)	83
Aidan Regan (10)	83
Rhys Arlow (10)	84
Craig Kincaid (9)	84

Natalie Chan (9)   85
Sarah Hunter (10)   85
Dylan McGunnigle (10)   86
Evan McQuillan (10)   86
Lee Alexander Donald (10)   87
Liam Hare (10)   87
Cameron Henry (10)   88
Chelsi Buchan (9)   88
Sean Wilkie (10)   89
Rhys Evans (10)   89
Sophie McCormick (9)   89
Drew Hepburn (10)   90
Caragh Jamison (9)   90
Steven Donald (8)   91
Rebecca Heron & Euan Hare (9)   91
Samantha Woods   92
Kyra Copeland (9)   92
Kayleigh Turner (9)   92
Ryan Harper (9)   93
Chloe Munro (9)   93
Megan Ruddy (9)   93
Megan Felgate (9)   94
Annabel Black (9)   94
Cara Cunningham (9)   94

Richmond Park School, Glasgow
Harry Mackie (11)   95
Michael Love (11)   95
Kieran Boult (11)   95
Gemma McGowan (10)   96
Ramzan Akram (10)   96
Gerard McQuade (11)   97

St Agnes' Primary School, Glasgow
Charlotte Reilly (9)   97
Anna Shields (11)   98
Sophy McAloon (8)   98
Tasha Gilmartin (8)   98
Shannon Hamilton (9)   99

St Cadoc's Primary School, Newton Mearns

Caitlin Fitzpatrick (11)	99
Ewan Forsyth (11)	99
Isla Nosratzadeh (10)	100
Brogan Bennett (11)	100
Christopher McNulty (10)	101
Liam King (10)	101
Joe Devine (11)	102
Sara Stevenson (11)	102
Hannah Duffy (11)	103
Ryan Higgins (10)	103
James Duncan (11)	104
John Connor (10)	105
Nicola Ormiston (11)	106
Laura Connelly (10)	107
Shahad Hilmy (11)	108

St Mark's Primary School, Edinburgh

Kayleigh Eddington (10)	108
Aimee Moore (10)	109
Stuart Lockhart (9)	109
Georgia Daisy Hill (9)	110
Tiffany Wilson (9)	110
Amie McIntosh (9)	110
Stephen Pearson (9)	111
Hannah Gibbons (8)	111
Nicolle Sims (9)	111
Caitlin Mackay (9)	112
Callum Costello (9)	112
Owen Duddy (9)	112
Beth Coxon (8)	113
John Harvey (8)	113
Lucie Broadbent (8)	113
Shaun MacFarlane (11)	114
Aidan Haughey (9)	114
Stuart Cockin (11)	115
Jonathan Robertson (8)	115
Evie Kircos (11)	116
Samuel Murray (10)	116
Cameron Cunnea (10)	117
Kieran Davies (10)	117

Peter Connelly (11)   118
Naomi Baird (11)   118
Nico Colarusso (10)   119
Sean Melville (11)   119
Aidan Duddy (11)   120
Sinead Blyth (11)   120
Chloe Hannant (10)   121
Emily Berri (10)   121
Erin Kennedy (10)   122
Daniel Kinghorn (11)   122
Louise Doyle (11)   123
Jacob Curran (10)   123
Hollie Charleston (10)   124

St Mary's Primary School, Greenock

Harry Dyer (9)   124
Jamie Millar (10)   125
Matthew Skilling (10)   125
Daire Coyle (9)   126
Matthew Fulton (10)   126
Christy Forbes (9)   127
Nicole Bradley (10)   127
Callum McDade (9)   128
Stephen Kane (11)   128
Charlie McCartney (10)   129
Lauren Robinson (10)   129
Charis Jackson (10)   130
Caryn Mearns (10)   130
Megan Clark (11)   131
Rachael Robertson (11)   131
Gianluca Porceddu (11)   132
Courtney Patton (10)   132
Iona Gisbey (10)   133
Aidan Watt (10)   133
Heather Ramsay (10)   134
Stephen Daisley (9)   134
Robyn Wilson (11)   135
Ainsley Brennan   136
Rebecca Keane (11)   136
Connor McLeod (11)   137
Siobhan R Riddoch (11)   137

Dominic Jack (10)	138
Paul Dorrian (11)	138
Nina Hughes (10)	139

Slaemuir Primary School, Port Glasgow

Lianna Marshall (10)	139
Shannon Archibald (10)	140
Toni McCluskey (10)	140
Lucy Ballingall (10)	141
Thomas McMath (10)	141
Alistair McMath (10)	142
Josh Lochrie (10)	142
Chloe Lowry (9)	142
Christopher Coumparoules (10)	143
Andrew McMath (11)	143
Lewis Macleod (10)	143
Hayley Williamson (10)	144
Fraser Tracey (10)	144
Jack Attfield (9)	144
Karla Coyle (10)	145
Steven McCulloch (10)	145
Lee Marshall (10)	145

The Poems

Christmas Acrostic Poem

C hristmas trees are getting decorated, jingly bells and all.
H aving fun all day and night.
R udolph is getting ready to shine his big red nose.
I f you hear a ho ho ho you'll know he is here.
S anta's little helpers are making all the presents.
T owns are getting decorated, pictures of Santa and more.
M aybe if you're lucky you might even see the big red man.
A s soon as Christmas strikes, you'll feel a magical tingle
S anta's here, he has just said, 'Ho ho ho merry Christmas and a
    happy New Year.'

Callum Laing & Ian Robinson (9)
Amisfield Primary School, Dumfries

Spooky Cemetery

At the dark spooky cemetery
On hot Bonfire Night
In the screaming haunted house
The ghostly golden cave is full of vampires
Below the haunted hill
A lake of crocodiles are ready to eat you all up
And branch breaking woods with goblins.

Alex Stewart (9) & Ross Green (7)
Amisfield Primary School, Dumfries

Rugby

Passing the ball across the pitch
It might be sunny or it might be rainy
Someone gets a free kick or a penalty
He scores a try!

Owen Stewart & Thomas Marshall (8)
Amisfield Primary School, Dumfries

Bonfire At The Woods

One time in the woods it was Bonfire Night.
They got scared because they started to hear things,
In the spooky woods they heard rats crawling around.
Then they started to wonder where they were.
They smelt soggy mud.
When they were walking it started to stick to them,
Then they heard branches snapping.
When they touched the rotten tree it started to crumble.

Lauren Johnstone & Helen Burgess (8)
Amisfield Primary School, Dumfries

Scorpions

Scorpions have a sting in their tail
Don't go too near or you'll go pale.
Scorpions have big, sharp claws
Humans don't give them a round of applause.
They are black, they are white,
They will give you a big fright.
They sometimes misbehave,
They sometimes live in a cave.
They are edible,
Some people think they are incredible.

Jacob Bohill (9)
Bishopton Primary School, Bishopton

Hunger

Hunger is blue like a raging ocean.
Hunger sounds like groans from the dead.
Hunger tastes like an empty cupboard.
Hunger looks like a bare table.
Hunger smells like cooking food in the oven.
Hunger feels like an empty stomach.
Hunger reminds me of starving people.

Mark Smith (9)
Bishopton Primary School, Bishopton

Flowers

Flowers are wonderful, happy and bright.
Flowers light up the world at night.
Flowers bloom very light.
Flowers are a happy sight.
Flowers smell very sweet.
Flowers are lovely and neat.
Flowers make you feel like having fun.
Flowers are fun for everyone.
Flowers are good so show some love.
Flowers are nature, nature like us.

Kerry-Ellen Fleming (9)
Bishopton Primary School, Bishopton

Fun

Fun is blue like a calm sea.
Fun sounds like happy kids.
Fun tastes like sweet cake.
Fun smells like birthday cake candles.
Fun feels like you're as free as a newborn bird.
Fun reminds me of happy times.

Rob Wallace (9)
Bishopton Primary School, Bishopton

Happiness

Happiness is bright blue like the sky
It feels like the touch of a leopard's skin
It sounds like rap music
It tastes like chocolate ice cream
It looks like a colourful rainbow
It smells like chocolate cake
It reminds me of my soft pillow.

Liam Russell (7)
Bishopton Primary School, Bishopton

Anger

Anger is red like flames coming off a building
It feels like a sharp, jaggy nettle
It sounds like a car crashing
It tastes like burning toast
It smells like rotten apples
It looks like a car crashing with flames
It reminds me of a lion.

Gregor Edwards (8)
Bishopton Primary School, Bishopton

Fear

Fear is black like a horrible Rottweiler
It feels like touching a slug
It sounds like someone screaming
It smells like a roaring fire
It tastes like a horrible worm
It looks like a horrible bug
It reminds me of a horror film.

Calum Clark (8)
Bishopton Primary School, Bishopton

Sadness

Sadness is blue like the pale blue sky
It feels like a slimy slug
It sounds like someone crying
It tastes like rotten carrots
It smells like onions
It looks like a dead body
It reminds me of when I fell.

Iona MacPherson (8)
Bishopton Primary School, Bishopton

Happiness

Happiness is bright yellow like the sunshine
It feels like my favourite soft toy
It tastes like chocolate
It sounds like birds singing
It smells like cake straight out of the oven
It looks like a newborn baby
It reminds me of my pet cat.

David Watt (8)
Bishopton Primary School, Bishopton

Happiness

Happiness is bright yellow like a summer's sun
It feels like fur of a newborn puppy
It sounds like a cat purring on my lap
It tastes like home-made chocolate cake
It smells like a newborn baby
It looks like a vase of flowers
It reminds me of my sister.

Jordan Alex Lamb (7)
Bishopton Primary School, Bishopton

Happiness

Happiness is bright like the yellow sunshine
It feels like silky pyjamas
It sounds like people laughing
It tastes like chocolate ice cream
It looks like a beautiful rainbow
It smells like lovely cooking
It reminds me of seeing the lovely blue sky.

Heather Munro (8)
Bishopton Primary School, Bishopton

Love

Love is like the bright yellow sun
It feels like a soft, fluffy dog
It sounds like soft music
It tastes like melted chocolate
It looks like a fluffy cushion
It smells like chocolate
It reminds me of my mum.

Drew Munro (8)
Bishopton Primary School, Bishopton

Autumn Poem

Dead leaves falling from the trees quietly and gently, huge moss trees
Like big green giants.
Small brambles ready for eating
Lots of cones, big and spiky,
Cracking twigs off the trees, muddy ground squidgy and sticky.

Leaves crackling in the wind
Rain dropping in the puddles, making sounds like wet fish jumping
Footsteps thumping and bumping
People talking, cones breaking when being stood on.

The damp earth that smells worse than an elephant
Juicy brambles ready to eat
Damp nature after all the rain and the scent of new flowers.

Nature all around me
Sweet flowers and the sweet taste of sour brambles
That makes my mouth water.

The bark of the tree which is really hard and wrinkly
The moss all soft and squidgy.

Kind of happy and kind of sad
Because winter is near which means Christmas is near too
And sad because summer is gone and school is back.

Keith MacDonald (10)
Bowmore Primary School, Bowmore

Autumn Is Great

In autumn there are lots of brambles to eat
they taste like sour sweets.
And there are lots of leaves falling from trees
like paratroopers jumping from an aeroplane.

There are lots of mini helicopters in autumn
and trees in the woods.

There are lots of conkers in the woods
they are like mini houses on the ground.
You can see the trees' leaves die
there are lots of leaves.

You can smell the fresh air of the woods.
You can play with the mini helicopters.
You can play games in the woods.

There are lots of things to do in the woods
you can climb trees and play hide-and-seek.
In the woods you can play with the leaves
the woods is a great place to be in autumn.

Liam MacDougall (10)
Bowmore Primary School, Bowmore

My Autumn Poem

Old dying leaves falling off trees
Crunchy crispy twigs, natural flowers
Crinkly old leaves shining bright
Geese singing as beautifully as a choir.

Damp earth as sticky as toffee.
Brambles as sour as a lemon,
Pine cones as prickly as hedgehogs
Sticks as hard as rock.

Sad summer has gone and winter is near.

Connor Louis Boyd (10)
Bowmore Primary School, Bowmore

Autumn Poem

The tree's life depends on its leaves,
There is no sound of the leaves falling off the trees.
All there is is the sound of the birds singing
And the mud squelching as you walk through it,
Even though you wouldn't plan to.

As the leaves change colour, it means they are dying
And they fall off the trees and just stay there lying.
As they lie, they fade away, some get eaten by other animals,
Some rot into the ground, that's all they do until autumn ends.

Autumn smells like mint, lime, ink and moss
It also smells like burnt wood, (lead mostly).
It tastes like mint and it makes you feel like a frozen ice cube.

Joe-Lewis McKirdy (10)
Bowmore Primary School, Bowmore

Autumn

Falling leaves softly falling to the ground with a rustle
And cold rain dropping off the leaves.

Rustling echoing through the woods
And animals calling to each other.

Damp, woody, nature smell coming from the woods.

Sour brambles as tasty as really sour sweets.

Thorny bushes and crinkled leaves
Also rain falling into your hand.

Thrilled because you can hear red deer calling
Geese calling as well.

Andrew Bauld (9)
Bowmore Primary School, Bowmore

Beautiful Autumn

The crinkled dying leaves fluttering down like little parachutes
Brambles turning purple from green
Conkers smooth like silk

Rain gently falling on the wet muddy ground like calming music
Geese echoing in the cool autumn sky, they sound tired and hungry

No longer the smell of summer flowers,
It smells cold and damp like an old house
Dull and mouldy
Taste all the juicy fruits
Sugar rots your teeth
Monkey nuts, yum-yum

Touch the moss soft as a rug
Lichen spotty on the trees

I love autumn and all the lovely colours
Things die but new things grow back in summer.

Rachael Armour (10)
Bowmore Primary School, Bowmore

Autumn!

Softly golden leaves lying on the ground in the woods.
Raindrops falling as loud as a drum.

The dampness on the muddy ground.
The taste of the powerful dampness.

Leaves like a rug
I feel really bad because summer is at an end
Winter is just round the corner.

Sorcha Dewar (11)
Bowmore Primary School, Bowmore

Awesome Autumn

Falling leaves fluttering like fairies,
Trees as spiky as a hedgehog.
Conkers as smooth as Minstrels,
And slugs as slimy as the slaver of a dog!

Raindrops dripping from the bare branches,
Leaves rustling like crunchy crisps.
Twigs snapping like breaking a leg,
With birds singing peacefully like opera singers.

A fusty smell in the air,
Like jam on burned toast.
Damp air, warm and sweaty,
As if there's a sweaty ghost!

Bramble juice, bursting into flavour,
Like summer fruits juice.
As sour as a sour sucker,
Tiny pips as annoying as a goose!

Mouldy bark as mushy as peas,
Wet grass as it wets your knees!
I feel sorry that summer is over,
But good that Christmas is near.

Ashley Harrison (11)
Bowmore Primary School, Bowmore

Beautiful Autumn

In the wood, leaves falling like feathers in the little wind.

Wee rain quiet as a mouse pattering on the trees.

Fresh grass smells more beautiful than anything.

Juicy brambles soft like cotton wool.

The rough leaves like very, very old trees.

Autumn makes me sad because winter is coming for a long time.

Paulina Bialka (10)
Bowmore Primary School, Bowmore

My Autumn Poem

Dying red leaves gently falling onto the squelchy, boggy ground,

The big tall trees starting to grow bald,
Conkers dying and the small pine cones.

Geese softly singing from above in the nice blue sky
Lots of brown, long and short twigs loudly snapping.

Damp air and crinkled old leaves.

Black tasty brambles all fresh from the spiky bushes.

Sticky conkers falling from the trees and the small, hard pine cones.

I feel sad that summer is over and winter is near.

Ruairidh Scott (10)
Bowmore Primary School, Bowmore

Autumn Sweet Autumn

The sight of crinkled, old, dead leaves fluttering in the breeze
Like sparkly little fairies.

The sound of geese arrive for the winter blues
As loud as garage music.

The smell of the damp, wet earth
As smelly as an elephant.

The taste of sour brambles fills my mouth as they enter
As sour as a sour sucker.

The touch of hard conkers
As hard as a plane.

I feel sad and happy because old things die
But new things will be born soon.

Kirsty Harrison (10)
Bowmore Primary School, Bowmore

My Autumn Poem

The crinkly, dead leaves,
Falling to the soft, sticky ground,
Like little men with parachutes.
The small spiky conkers lying on the ground.
Like little medieval maces.
The old, dead leaves on the ground,
And when stood on,
Like a carpet of cornflakes.
The seeds of the sycamore,
Falling to the ground,
Like little helicopters.

The sound of geese,
Echoing through the autumn air.
Leaves hitting the ground,
Like little fairies,
Fluttering in the breeze.

The smell of the damp crumbly moss
And wet gooey ground.

The taste of juicy fruits
Such as apples or plums
Or the sour, black brambles.

The feeling of the rough bark
On the trees so tall.

I feel sad that the warmth of the summer has gone
But am happy that it will come again next year.

Christopher Corbett (10)
Bowmore Primary School, Bowmore

Autumn Woods

Dead trees sway from side to side
Like a boat in the sea
Moss crawling up trees
Like a spider
Leaves falling from trees
Like fluttering butterflies

Snapping sticks from the ground
Sound like snapping crocodiles
Honking from geese
Sound like car horns
Rain hitting off leaves
Sounding like lightning

The smell of moss
Is very damp
The dead leaves
Have the smell of bark
The smell of flowers
Starts to die

The sourness of brambles
Tastes like a sour ball
The juicy apples
Is like being in a shower of juice
The purple plums
Look like grapes

I feel excited and I feel upset about autumn
I feel excited because it is close to my birthday
I feel sad because I won't be able to stay down in Bowmore
For that long because it is getting darker.

Thomas Aitchison (10)
Bowmore Primary School, Bowmore

The Feelings Of Autumn

The fluttering leaves fall to the ground when you look up
They look like feathers falling from Heaven
When you look down you see a carpet of leaves
As red as the red carpet that famous people walk down.

A whirlwind of midges trying to eat you alive,
Worse than a swarm of bees when you disturb their beehive,
The bare trees look like fingers trying to catch the birds,
Their thin twigs that stick from branches
Look like a witch's broom end.

As you stand on the twigs that lie on the ground
They make a crack, bang, pop, it's a very strange sound.
You can also hear the geese honking all day
That sound like a car horn beeping away

You can smell the damp earth
That smells like the peat moss
That my dad makes me work in
He must think he is my boss.

You can taste brambles,
That taste like sour fruit
Not the kind of sour smell that comes
From my dad's welly boots.

When you touch the crusty leaves
They feel like a bag of crisps that have been
Crunched up and stuck back together.
The spiky pine cones
Feel like a hedgehog that has fallen out a tree
That has been knocked out the tree by the autumn breeze.

In a way I love autumn because of the nice walks you can
Have in the woods and it won't be too hot or too cold.
But some things die . . .

Jennifer McColl (10)
Bowmore Primary School, Bowmore

Autumn Poem

Multicoloured leaves
That have fallen onto the ground
Swarms of flies buzzing around
Like dark clouds.

The leaves are rustling when I walk through them
Geese are calling loudly
Like a marching band
And the rain is hitting off the trees furiously.

The damp smell of moss and bark
The lovely smell of brambles
Makes you hungry.

The taste of brambles
Makes you want more
Toffee apples getting stuck in my teeth
Boiled sweets taste so sweet.

Twigs on the ground feel
As dry as a desert
Leaves feel as crispy as crisps.

I'm feeling sad because
Summer has gone but
Happy because winter
Is just round the corner.

George Hathaway (11)
Bowmore Primary School, Bowmore

Autumn Poem

Bare trees swaying in the cold autumn wind
Fire-coloured leaves crunching on the ground
Brambles on their bushes just waiting to be picked
Moss covering up trees like they've been painted green.

Rain spluttering against the trees
Leaves crisping on the ground
Making a horrible crunching sound.

The smell of cut grass hanging in the air
And fresh air as fresh as ever.

Ripe apples as fresh as you can get
Brambles tasting very bitter.

Conkers feel as smooth as velvet
Leaves as soggy as vinegar on chips.

I feel happy because there are less midges
And sad because winter is near.

Frazer Matthews (11)
Bowmore Primary School, Bowmore

Favourite Things

My favourite sport is basketball.
When I score a basket,
I cheer with my backwards roll.

My favourite food is chicken.
I cook it when it's kickin'
I have it with bread or chips
And I'm now licking my lips.

Winter is the best season of all.
I build igloos, then watch them fall.
I knock people's snowmen down.
And watch their faces, as they frown.

Gregor Cooper (10)
Drymen Primary School, Glasgow

Seasons

Winter is the time of year with snow
Snowballs I really like to throw
In winter it really does get cold
In layers of clothes I like to mould.

Spring is the time of year with flowers
And I could smell the scent for hours
When I look up at all the trees
Their greenery amazes me.

Summer is the time of year with lots of sun
And I always have loads of fun
My dad sits on the long pier
Sitting and drinking loads of beer.

Autumn is the time of year when leaves start to fall
But when they get to the ground they seem small
There is also a scary Hallowe'en
And when I go outside people scream.

Jake Marshall (10)
Drymen Primary School, Glasgow

Favourite Things

Tractors are vehicles big and strong
They can pull trailers very long

The Ferrari and the Lambo fly
And the Aston Martin speeds by.

My family it's the absolute best
They can way beat all the rest.

Kickboxing is the way to fight
And it's effective if you do it right.

Tractors, cars, family and fight
I love these things with all my might.

James Findlay (10)
Drymen Primary School, Glasgow

Favourite Things

C is for chunky that's how I like it,
H is for hard until it melts,
O is for ouch, I think I bit my tongue,
C is for cartoons, it goes great with them,
O is for outside, it melts out there,
L is for loopy it makes some people,
A is for ahh, that's good,
T is for tasty, oh so yummy,
E is for eating the chocolate,
S is for sweet, I love it so much.

F is for florists, the ones who arrange them,
L is for lovely, well I think they are,
O is for outside where most live,
W is for wonderful, they look so good,
E is for excellent, the way they get arranged,
R is for roses, one of my favourite,
S is for smelly, *not* the bad type.

K is for keen, keen to eat,
O is for outrageous, awesomely cool,
A is for awesome, just like my friends,
L is for lovely I love them so much,
A is for asleep, they do that for 18 hours,
S is for so cute, they are so cute.

Annabelle Ferguson (10)
Drymen Primary School, Glasgow

Seasons

In spring I like to pick flowers,
In spring I clean for hours and hours.
Newborn animals come to life,
All over the world, even Fife.

In summer the hot sun shines,
I drink lemonade, my parents drink wine.
I think holidays are really fun,
Me and my brother frolic in the sun.

Autumn is the time when leaves fall,
On the window ledge and the hall.
Red, yellow, orange and brown,
Into the jungle and all over town.

In winter Christmas comes,
I get presents from Dad and Mum.
Snow falls down and down and down,
All the way to the ground.

As bright as a fire the sun shines,
First it rains then the next day it's fine.
My favourite seasons are summer and spring,
I love them both, I hear my heart sing.

Kirsten McCabe (10)
Drymen Primary School, Glasgow

Seasons

There are four seasons in the year
Bringing different noises that we hear
Different seasons with rain or sun
Always bringing lots of fun

Spring is when the leaves are green
Baby animals can be seen
Weather changing all the time
Farmers come in at night to dine

Summer, when we are at the seaside
Children running as fast as the tide
The sea as blue as a sapphire
Lots of people sit back and admire

Autumn brings us Hallowe'en
The scary costumes make you scream
Leaves as orange as a fire
Lots of fireworks that we desire

Winter when the trees are bare
The snow is crossed by a galloping hare
The soft and fluffy cotton wool snow
And the slush that makes a river flow

Seasons slide past like a soft stream
They are almost like a gentle dream
Seasons come and seasons go
Some go fast, others go slow.

Jan Duncan (10)
Drymen Primary School, Glasgow

The Seasons

In spring out come all the flowers,
Spring cleaning always takes hours,
In spring animals are born,
In the field there's a galloping fawn.

Summer, summer, what a glorious time,
In the evening adults drink wine,
In the summer I go abroad,
There you will find me on a surfboard.

In autumn there are crispy leaves,
Farmers gathering in all sheaves,
Yellow, red, orange, brown,
Autumn colours lie all around.

In the winter you get crackling fires,
In the sales there are lots of buyers,
Stars like diamonds in the sky,
Best of all is home-made mince pie.

Seasons, seasons,
All year round,
They're all different,
So I've found.

Jamie Hall (9)
Drymen Primary School, Glasgow

Favourite Things

My favourite sport is football,
You can play if you're tall or small.
Every time I score a goal,
I celebrate with a forward roll.

Christmas is my favourite season,
There is no particular reason.
Except to sing carols under a tree,
And put up the star, so sparkly.

Cheese is my favourite food,
Although most of the time it needs to be cooled.
Brie, Cheddar, double Gloucester too,
But my favourite would have to be blue.

Mum, Dad, my brother Sam,
Aunt, Uncle and my gran.
All the time I love them lots,
Even when we go to the shops.

All these things, I think are great,
Football, cheese, I can't wait.

Josh Degg (9)
Drymen Primary School, Glasgow

Seasons

Winter is the coldest season
Icicles hanging, adults freezing
When the snow falls the children slip
And on the hidden branches they sometimes trip.

Spring is the time when the lambs dance
All the horses and foals gallop and prance
Sun or rain, I really don't care
But I really don't know what to wear.

Summer is the greatest season
Always out for no reason
The weather, it is so hot
You play and play until you drop.

Autumn is really fun
On Hallowe'en
Scary faces make us scream and scream
Autumn is colourful believe
Because of all the orange, brown and gold leaves.

David Johnstone (10)
Drymen Primary School, Glasgow

Seasons

Autumn is the time when the leaves all fall,
Right into your window and into your hall
My cousin Blair got a new pup,
He's scattered the leaves, I must pick them up.

Winter is when the snow's like wool
It's certainly not time for the pool
Snow's as white as white can be
It's stretched as far as I can see.

Spring's the time for you to clean,
My mum's been cleaning I have seen
Lots of lambs are born in spring
Do some of them have ankle rings?

Summer is the time for you to have fun
In your front and back gardens in the hot sun
I go on lots of holidays
I only wish that I could stay.

Cameron O'Donnell
Drymen Primary School, Glasgow

Seasons

See some sheep have their lambs
As the others lick your palms
Then see the flowers lighten up
Like a colourful teacup.

Now that summer's come
Let's all have some fun
We go and visit the Japanese
From our summer holidays.

I am playing with my ball
As I see the colourful leaves fall
Hooray! Autumn's come out
Let's throw the fallen leaves about.

Out there the weather is so cold
Everyone is freezing, I'm told
Looks like it's wintertime
Rejoice, let's all have some wine!

Lewis Strachan (10)
Drymen Primary School, Glasgow

Environment

Our environment from the sky to the ground,
Is a sight to see, so look around.

Over snow-covered mountains,
Like a shining crown
The sun beamed brightly,
A golden brown.

By the river rippling of water
And the fish quickly dart by.
The wild flapping of wings,
The seagulls' familiar cry.

Into the forest the smell of pine,
Sweetens the air, simply divine.
The wise old oak with secrets to tell,
Ash, beech and chestnut as well.

The rolling hills where wildlife dwells,
Is the only place that honesty tells.
The secrets of the natural world
And the bracken, brown and curled.

All the nature, small and tall,
Is what's beyond the garden wall.

Zoë Glen (10)
Drymen Primary School, Glasgow

The Seasons

In spring there are mostly blue skies,
But then it says its last goodbyes
In spring you're in your garden for hours and hours
Because there are beautiful new flowers.

In summer you look round the land
It seems to turn into sand
On holiday you go to the seaside
And there we run from the tide.

In autumn the leaves are brown
And they scatter right through the town
In autumn you get in a muddle
When you splash in a puddle.

In winter you tread through the snow
And when you trip, you hurt your toe
In winter you can't see the trees
In the snow you lose keys.

Ruth Hurley (9)
Drymen Primary School, Glasgow

Favourite Things

Dogs cute and cuddly
Outside playing in the garden
Gorgeous fur and lovely
Sweet dogs.

Netball is sporty
Netball is fun
You pass and defend and you shoot a basket.

Football is fun
In football you score goals
You can watch it on TV
You can play it 5-a-side
You can play it in any number.

When you shop you drop
Shopping for clothes
Shopping for jewellery
Shopping for anything is fun.

Aimee Bourbousson (10)
Drymen Primary School, Glasgow

Seasons

Sitting in the sun having lots of fun.
Watching other people eat their creamy buns.
Out in the lovely seaside.
Looking into the window inside.

Flower scents in the fresh air
As the gentle breeze blows through my hair.
Watch the ewes having their lambs.
As the other lambs lick your palms.

I go to the beautiful mall.
As I watch all the golden-brown leaves fall.
I am inside now watching people put leaves in the bin.
I am sitting here watching them grin.

All the colourful leaves turn brown.
As I am starting to feel down.
But still it is fun watching people go into the cold.
But in here by the fire I fold.

Robyn Gemmell
Drymen Primary School, Glasgow

Environment

Cream-coloured cows chewing the cud.
Silly sheep slowly shirking the mud.
Farmers are pleased all year through.
Then sheep shows come, grooming to do.

As the cold north wind blows.
All the oak trees still grow.
People see the colourful leaves
Swaying in the calm breeze.

As night draws, the full moon appears.
Wolves come out howling their cheers.
Children doze off in their beds.
As the wolves prowl round their sheds.

In our environment there's lots to see.
Every butterfly, every bee.
Every ocean, every sea.

Louise Wright
Drymen Primary School, Glasgow

Crossing The River

Be careful crossing the river!
There lives a muddy hippo.
Be careful crossing the river!
There lives a long snake.
Be careful crossing the river!
There lives a deadly piranha.
Be careful crossing the river!
There lives a scaly crocodile.
Be careful crossing the river!
There lives a see-through jellyfish.

Max Carter (7)
Flora Stevenson Primary School, Edinburgh

Flying

I dream that one day I will fly,
I'll soar across the sky,
Through the white fluffy clouds,
With no thoughts.

I'll fly with a wonderful feeling,
Which makes everyone happy,
I'll fly to my heart's content.

I will race the birds,
Beat the sparrows,
But the eagles will beat me.

What a wonderful feeling,
Flying truly is.

Sophia Madden (10)
Flora Stevenson Primary School, Edinburgh

Unforetold Dreams

Dragons flying in the sky
While sports cars are driving by.
Dreams are where all your wishes come true

Aeroplanes flying and coming to land
While you are singing in a rock band.
In your dreams you can't feel blue

But as the day comes from night
And the sun starts to shine bright
Your dreams will fade until another night.

Harriet Johnston (9)
Flora Stevenson Primary School, Edinburgh

Star Wars

'Luke, it's Darth Vader
Quick turn on your lightsaber!'
The guns all pound
A lot of sound.
Yoda is ill!
He is very still,
Obi-Wan and Maul
Fighting in the big hall.
The clones have won
They have a big gun!
The Rebels are new in the war,
They are getting more and more!
The Emperor is great,
But he only has one mate!
The Ewoks are hiding
The scouts are riding!
Padme's now got Leia and Luke
And then they started to puke!
Luke is Leia's twin brother
But sadly they have lost their mother
Then their father had turned bad
So it made the twins *very* sad!
Now the Emperor has lost his mate!
They all started to celebrate!
Yoda, Ben and Anakin are ghosts,
So now the Rebels need to find new hosts.

Arran Mackintosh (7)
Flora Stevenson Primary School, Edinburgh

The Very Place I Long To Be

The very place I long to be
Is next to an old oak tree
With flowers growing beside me
And bunnies jumping all around
This is the place that someone found.

The very place I long to be
Is at home watching TV
I feel relaxed and it takes my troubles away
So I can live another day.

David McFarlan (11)
Flora Stevenson Primary School, Edinburgh

My Best Friend!

She's a bouncy ball,
Jumping up and down,
She's a monkey,
Wearing a gown,

She's kind,
She's funny,
She's out of her mind,
She's cool,
She's red,
She's danger,
She's my friend,
Rhianne.

Emma Clouston (10)
Flora Stevenson Primary School, Edinburgh

Imagination

A light goes off outside my brain,
But inside it goes on again,
It's this special time of day,
When my imagination comes out to play,
I'm that funny sort of child,
That lets my brain run free and wild,
But sometimes my imagination goes too far,
I'm on a road under a car,
Or sinking in a pool of mud,
Knife in my hand I'm covered in blood,
But sometimes my imagination runs free and calm,
I was not there, I did no harm.

Anna McLuckie (11)
Flora Stevenson Primary School, Edinburgh

Bully Rap!

Bullies bully you every day,
You get it for being different in any way,
You get it for being small or tall or even fat,
You even get it for having a cat,
At break you have your snack,
But the bullies take away your KitKat,
When the bell rings you tell the teacher,
Just go quickly make sure you see her,
The teacher sees the bullies and tells them off,
The next thing you know he's scared of a moth!

Max Law (10)
Flora Stevenson Primary School, Edinburgh

Blue

Blue is the ocean
Blue is the sky
Blue is blueberries
Blue is the beginning
Blue is Christmas
Blue is Chelsea
Blue sounds like rain, waterfalls and the ocean
Blue feels like you're calm, relaxed and cool
Blue makes me feel cool, cold and like the snow
Blue tastes like sweets, blueberries and juice
Blue is at the ocean, swimming pool, North Pole and waterfalls.
Blue is my favourite colour.

Lee Hunter (11)
Flora Stevenson Primary School, Edinburgh

Spooky

If my dreams were a person
They would be a killer cat
If they were a building
They would be a haunted house
My dreams are like scary dreams
Or they are like monsters
Dreams are sometimes silly and funny
Or sometimes spooky!

Freya Ruuskanen (7)
Flora Stevenson Primary School, Edinburgh

My Luck!

I had a dream I was out of luck
But then I won the lottery and bought a truck
I bought a house, I bought a pet
I bought a yacht, I bought a jet
I bought a mansion, I bought the sea
But that's not the man
I want to be.

Connor Sinclair (11)
Flora Stevenson Primary School, Edinburgh

Anger

It sounds like a scary beast roaring furiously.
It tastes like a pool of lava burning in my mouth painfully.
It smells like a glass of milk that has been lying out for days.
It looks like an old, scary, terrifying skeleton.
It feels like a pointy heavy rock being dropped on me.
It reminds me of lying in my bed one day and thinking about
the bad day I had.

Connor McArthur (11)
Foulford Primary School, Cowdenbeath

Fun

Fun is blue like the ocean.
Sounds like dolphins laughing
It tastes like sweets in your mouth.
It smells like the sea.
It looks like Heaven where everyone is laughing.
It feels like I am flying over the sea.
It reminds me of playing and having fun.

Pavinder Singh
Foulford Primary School, Cowdenbeath

Laughter

Laughter is a
big bang of blue
gigantic gunshots of green
everlasting, exploding red
all very vibrant

Laughter sounds like
continuous pops
exploding bangs
never-ending shrieks
all extremely raucous

Laughter tastes like
shooting sherbet
bubbling boiled sweets
fantasia fruits
big bursts of flavour

Laughter smells like
erupting mint
relaxing lavender
cool chamomile
wonderful fragrances

Laughter looks like
a tiger's tail swaying back and forth in the rushing
breeze of the wind
big blue polka dots on an orange background

Laughter feels like
extremely rough sandpaper
the trunk of a chestnut tree
a wiry coconut shell

Laughter reminds me of
when my dogs do something extremely funny
and highly amusing.

Conor Crichton (11)
Foulford Primary School, Cowdenbeath

Fun

Fun is a very bright yellow that is hearty and cheerful.
It sounds like a big party explosion.
It tastes as sweet as a candy cane.
It smells like a funfair.
It looks like children having a good time at the park.
It feels like you're on a roller coaster that goes upside down six times!
It reminds me of my 6th birthday party when I got a pink bouncy castle.

Nicole Menzies
Foulford Primary School, Cowdenbeath

Fun

Fun is a rainbow of colours, a firework just waiting to explode.
Fun sounds like the jingle of the ice cream van.
Fun tastes like the first big bite of ice cream melting in your mouth.
Fun smells like a cake just coming out of the oven.
Fun looks like big happy faces on balloons.
It feels like falling into a bundle of fur.
It reminds me of children laughing and having fun.

Dylan Stanton
Foulford Primary School, Cowdenbeath

Love

Love is red like a nice red rose
Love sounds like a soft floating harp
Love tastes like some soothing chocolates
you get on Valentine's Day
Love smells like a nice fragrant flower
covering a room with its lovely smell
Love looks like a long, blue, streaming waterfall
Love feels like a burning sensation in my heart
Love reminds me of being with my family and friends
and the time I spend with them.

Katie Wilson
Foulford Primary School, Cowdenbeath

Darkness

Darkness is a sickening black like a never-ending hole.
It sounds like a bullet shattering a window.
It tastes like bitter raw meat running down my mouth.
It smells like a dank room that you just walked into.
It looks like a raging bull going full speed at a red cape.
It feels like spiky scales thrusting into your heart.
It reminds me of my operation when I was three, it was scary.

Patrick Adamson (11)
Foulford Primary School, Cowdenbeath

Love

Love is pink like Cupid's loving heart,
Love sounds like a soft playing harp,
Love tastes like chocolate on Valentine's Day,
Love smells like roses tingling away,
Love looks like a shining star in the air,
Love feels like your heart is growing every second of the year,
Love reminds me of the romantic film, Romeo and Juliet.

Cara Scott
Foulford Primary School, Cowdenbeath

Silence

Silence is white like a curiously empty piece of paper,
Silence sounds like a light breeze of wind,
Silence tastes like salty tears running down my icy, damp cheeks,
Silence smells like heavy smoke rising to the rooftop,
Silence looks like an empty village waiting to be filled,
Silence feels like goosebumps prickly on my skin.
Shhhhh!

Amy Machray
Foulford Primary School, Cowdenbeath

Fun

Fun is yellow
like the sun or
is it a yellow
balloon filled with
Fun?

Fun sounds like
popcorn popping,
Balloons bursting,
Pop, pop, pop.

Fun tastes like
melted chocolate,
vanilla ice cream and
chocolate sauce.

Fun smells like
cakes and cookies
baking in the
oven.

Fun feels like
bouncing high
in the sky
on a huge
trampoline.

Fun looks like
a big yellow
smiley face running and
running like
it's a race.

Fun reminds me of
playing sports
and games
when I
was wee,
it was
fun!

Shaun Hunter (11)
Foulford Primary School, Cowdenbeath

Fear

Fear is as black as a black hole,
completely isolated and never-ending.

Fear sounds like a desperate scream,
a scream that will never be heard.

Fear tastes like a rotten egg,
always being spat out but never disposed of.

Fear smells like a wet dog,
completely awful and impossible to get rid of.

Fear looks like a shark-infested whirlpool,
a guarantee of a gruesome death.

Fear feels like a six-inch tarantula crawling up my face,
waiting to insert its venom.

Fear reminds me of falling from a plane,
if the altitude doesn't kill you the ground will.

Lewis Ratcliffe (10)
Foulford Primary School, Cowdenbeath

Happiness

Happiness is bright splashes of colours
like a meadow of beautiful flowers.

Happiness sounds like the splash of waves,
gently going back and forward against the golden sand.

Happiness tastes like the sweet flavour of fruitiness.

Happiness smells like the calming fragrance of striking flowers.

Happiness looks like a hot, tropical beach
With crystal water and golden shiny sand.

Happiness feels like a burst of excitement.
Happiness reminds me of water fights in the summer sun.

Louise
Foulford Primary School, Cowdenbeath

Fear

Fear is black like a hairy, venomous, exotic spider
never catching its prey

Fear sounds like a stormy sea bashing against rocks,
rocks that will never be seen wshhh

It tastes like an eel that has tried to be eaten
but it's impossible

It smells like a dead hyena rotting in the jungle
lying there for the past two months

It looks like a gigantic red dragon blowing flames,
flames that will be seen for miles

It feels like scraping your nails along rusted metal,
metal that's been in the rain for years

It reminds me of screams with an echo,
screams that will never be heard by a human.

Reece Sealey
Foulford Primary School, Cowdenbeath

Darkness!

Darkness is black,
as black as night, as black as coal.

It sounds empty, all hollow inside,
all you can hear is your heart beating with fear.

It tastes like grey smoke burning from a fire.

Darkness smells like a rusty old pipe covered in slippery oil.

Darkness feels like ice freezing on a child's delicate skin.

Darkness reminds me of death
And lots of sad things that have happened.

Nicole Wilkie (11)
Foulford Primary School, Cowdenbeath

Happiness

Happiness is yellow and red flowers in a flower bed.
Happiness sounds like the trees gently swaying in the wind.
Happiness tastes like freshly baked bread coming out of the oven.
Happiness smells like a red rose in a big vase.
Happiness looks like a rainbow bursting with colour.
Happiness feels like a soft pillow under my head.
Happiness reminds me of someone smiling.

Siobhan Maxwell
Foulford Primary School, Cowdenbeath

Hallowe'en!

Hallowe'en like you have never seen
Hallowe'en, Hallowe'en, oh I just love Hallowe'en
The dark sky scares us all
Thinking I saw a witch down my hall.
Scared to go out,
Just want to jump and run about!
Went to my neighbours first singing 'trick or treat, smell my feet
Give me something else to eat.'
After that I saw lots of bats on the tree
Staring right down at me!
All my friends having parties
Dancing with a bowl of Smarties
Saw an old cauldron down the hall
I guess the witch was down the mall.
I saw the witch back in the sky
Oh help me! I don't want to die!

Chiara Quadrelli (10)
John Paul II Primary School, Glasgow

Hallowe'en

It's Hallowe'en, it's Hallowe'en!
The moon is full and bright,
And we shall see what can't be seen
On any other night.

Skeletons, ghosts and ghouls,
Grinning goblins fighting duels,
Werewolves rising from their tombs,
Witches on their magic brooms.

Caitlyn Ward (10)
John Paul II Primary School, Glasgow

Autumn Days

Autumn days
Summer has passed,
Autumn's here at last,
Leaves are lying on the ground,
People all around,
Children having fun
In the autumn sun,
Summer has passed,
Autumn's here at last.

Laura Houston (10)
John Paul II Primary School, Glasgow

Hallowe'en

Hallowe'en, Hallowe'en, Hallowe'en
We get dressed up to be seen
Witches, wizards, vampires and ghosts
Come to my Hallowe'en party.
And I'll be the best host.

Reagan Petrie (7)
John Paul II Primary School, Glasgow

Hallowe'en

H appy children out trick or treating,
A ll dressed like ghosts,
L aughing and giggling,
L oudly and horribly,
O wls are hooting in trees,
W itches are cackling
E ating frogs' legs
E ven pigs' ears.
N ever go out on Hallowe'en!

Yasmin Shariff (10)
John Paul II Primary School, Glasgow

Hallowe'en Is Good

Hallowe'en is good
Hallowe'en is scary
Laugh like a witch
Act like a fairy

When the full moon comes out
The ghosts and ghouls come out tonight
Witches and werewolves give us a fright.

Happy scary Hallowe'en.

Shauna McAuley (9)
John Paul II Primary School, Glasgow

Hallowe'en

Hallowe'en, Hallowe'en is so scary.
Once I saw an ugly fairy.
Her face was yellow,
Her eyes were green.
Oh she really made me scream.
I turned around and ran away.
Very, very far away.

Megan McGregor (8)
John Paul II Primary School, Glasgow

Trick Or Treat

It's Hallowe'en come outside and play,
Children are screaming,
Witches making soup,
Ghosts are saying boo!
Wizards are making the most wonderful spells,
Cats are scratching too!
Owls are hooting,
Pumpkins light up the dark,
. . . so don't stay at home,
Come outside and trick or treat!

Thesia Kamba Banza (11)
John Paul II Primary School, Glasgow

Hallow's Eve

It's Hallowe'en, let's trick or treat,
The boys and girls will have lots to eat.
It's Hallowe'en, we'll have lots of fun,
Dressing up . . . hope you can run.
The witches are out, the ghosts are too,
They're all coming out to capture you!
It's Hallow's Eve the witches' night
So remember not to get a fright.
They're in the trees, they're in the skies
The spirits are out so shut your eyes.
If you see or if you hear
The cauldrons bubbling, they're very near.
Don't worry, you will be alright,
Just remember your pumpkin tonight!

Aeron Birney (11)
John Paul II Primary School, Glasgow

Happy Hallowe'en

H appy Hallowe'en to the Queen,
A ll the children are shouting and screaming,
L ots of ghosts and ghouls out tonight,
L ots of children getting a fright!
O ut comes the moon and you hear a howl,
W olves are scaring, the night is wearing,
E vil is about, everyone screams and shouts,
E verybody runs about,
N ever go out at Hallowe'en, 'cause zombies are about!

Anthony McKinnon (11)
John Paul II Primary School, Glasgow

Autumn

The golden leaves fall off the old trees.
The golden leaves lie under the trees.
The leaves change colour because it's not summer.
It's cold, not hot as the sun
Is not here to play,
It's gone away.

The trees look bare.
The branches swaying,
As I was saying
Autumn is here,
Summer no more.
It's not hot anymore.

While the clouds are out.
The children are not.

Kimberly Houghton (10)
John Paul II Primary School, Glasgow

Hallowe'en, Hallowe'en

H appy Hallowe'en.
A costume is needed.
L et's scare the neighbours.
L et's get treats.
O r we will trick you.
W itches, wizards and monsters.
E veryone has fun.
E veryone gets candy and sweets.
N ever had such fun.

Andrew Duffin (7)
John Paul II Primary School, Glasgow

Hallowe'en Night

H allowe'en is a scary time,
A ll the children dress up at night,
L ots of children get a fright,
L ook out for witches and ghosts!
O h look, it's the wizard's toast,
W hen the moon is full,
E vil creatures come out,
E verybody screams and shouts,
N ever go out on Hallowe'en night!

Jay Kelly (10)
John Paul II Primary School, Glasgow

Hallowe'en!

H allowe'en is a scary time
A really spooky time
L ots of people dress up
L ook out ghosts and witches about
O h! I think I heard some groaning
W hen the ghosts see you they'll haunt you
E vil green, fat goblins sneaking
E very pumpkin glowing in the night
N ever ever go out at Hallowe'en again!

Jamie-Leigh Walker (10)
John Paul II Primary School, Glasgow

Hallowe'en, Hallowe'en

Hallowe'en, Hallowe'en
It is a scary scene
If you see a ghost with red eyes
Then you'd better say your goodbyes
I once saw a ghost
Who was scarier than most
So I said, 'Don't boast!'
Kiddies eating their sweeties
Not knowing what's behind them
Out pops a witch
Who scares them out of their wits.

Reece Montague (10)
John Paul II Primary School, Glasgow

The Ghosts

G hosts everywhere people screaming, ghosts
H owling, flying through the cold air, nobody knows where to
look next
O h, I'm soo . . . scared, I'm shaking in my bed
S cared, I'm going to be eaten up
T all scary witches, people already being eaten
S creaming during the night and giving myself a fright.

Megan Keenan (10)
John Paul II Primary School, Glasgow

Hallowe'en

H allowe'en is coming
A ll the wee kiddies are running
L arge spiders all about
L ittle kiddies want to scream and shout
O h, look up! Look up! Look up to the sky
W itches give out a frightening cry!
E vil zombies fast asleep
E vening comes, they're on their feet
N ight-night children, don't you cry,
shut your windows so you don't die!

Nathan Flanagan (10)
John Paul II Primary School, Glasgow

Skeleton

S cary monsters all around
K iddies screaming at the sound
E ating worms and spider eyes
L istening to the ghostly cries!
E vil witches taking flight
T hrough the cold and icy night
O h how can this be true?
N ow I'm really frightened too.

Michael Mutondoro (10)
John Paul II Primary School, Glasgow

Hallowe'en

H owl, howl all around, see the bodies on the ground.
A ll the bad and evil queens love the day called Hallowe'en.
L ook up at the sky at night, see the witches die with fright.
L oud they scream, away we go! While they're eating a hairy toe!
O wl, owl, can you hear?
W ee little kiddies scream in fear
E ating worms and blood they're drinking
E vil witches' eyes are blinking!
N ow the ghostly ships are sinking!

Jamie Downie (11)
John Paul II Primary School, Glasgow

Black Grace

On a still, frosty night
When the moon is bright
And all around is crisp and glistening
Out he trots and stops to look
To see if anyone is listening
He lifts his head and sniffs the air.
Out he steps from his hidden place.
A beautiful black horse who is full of grace.

Rebekah Weston (10)
John Paul II Primary School, Glasgow

Zombies Here

Z ombies, zombies everywhere
O h no, where's the mayor?
M aybe the zombies have got him
B eware of Zombie Tim
I am so scared like everyone else
E ven the eggs are jumping
S hivering cats. Shivering me!

Rebecca Morton (10)
John Paul II Primary School, Glasgow

The Hallowe'en Tale!

Ghosts are white
Pumpkins are orange
Hallowe'en gives everyone a big fright
And if a vampire ever bit you
You would turn into his slave
And look out for a full moon
Or you will see something in the wilderness and say
Argh! A werewolf! And never be seen again
And look out for the Grim Reaper
Frankenstein, and all the other things
I've said in this Hallowe'en tale!

And happy Hallowe'en!

Andrew Scott (10)
John Paul II Primary School, Glasgow

Hallowe'en

H appy Hallowe'en
A nd everybody is coming round doors.
L ike going trick or treating.
L et's have a Hallowe'en party.
O ooooow, it's spooky outside.
W aiting for others to come to the Hallowe'en party.
E veryone wants to tell a ghost story.
E veryone has told ghost stories.
N ow let's go trick or treating and have fun.

Shannon McNulty (9)
John Paul II Primary School, Glasgow

Hallowe'en

Phantoms here and witches there
Ghosts, ghosts, ghosts,
Vampires too
Hallowe'en will scare you, Boo!
Trick or treat but be careful who you meet
You don't know who's on the street.
Hallowe'en is here, full of fear.
What's that noise scaring all the girls and boys?
Witches flying, people are dying
And all their families are crying.
Hallowe'en is a scary time
Spiders crawling up your spine
Don't be scared it will be fine
Hallowe'en will give you tears
And it will go on for many years!

Sean O'Neill (10)
John Paul II Primary School, Glasgow

Hallowe'en, Hallowe'en

Hallowe'en, Hallowe'en
Doesn't it just want to make you scream?
First I ask trick or treat.
Then I tell a joke and get some sweets.
Or a treat to break your teeth.
Dressing as a witch is the costume I like the most.
While most of the boys like dressing as ghosts.

Lauryn Coyle (8)
John Paul II Primary School, Glasgow

Hallowe'en

H allowe'en, it's a spooky time,
A t night watch out! You will get a fright,
L ots of girls and boys dressing up as scary creatures,
L ook out! There are witches flying about.
O h, I think I heard a ghost groan and moan,
W izards and witches putting spells on you!
E vil goblins round and fat, coming to eat the rats,
E very pumpkin orange and round, lights up Hallowe'en night,
N ever go out at Hallowe'en ever again!

Jordyn Smith (11)
John Paul II Primary School, Glasgow

Hallowe'en

Hallowe'en, Hallowe'en
I dreamt I dressed up as the Queen for Hallowe'en.

There were lots of children on the street.
Looking for some trick or treats.
But children, please beware.
Because round the corner there could be a scare.

Witches, bats and big black cats.
Ghosts, ghouls and goblins too.

Oh how I loved being a queen.
And telling what I'd seen
In my Hallowe'en dream.

Laura Donnelly (8)
John Paul II Primary School, Glasgow

Hallowe'en

H aving fun on the very day.

A nd scarecrows are very scary.

L ong before Hallowe'en all the people say 'Boo!'

L aughing and screaming all day long.

O wls howl all night.

W itches make their way through the town.

E nd of day.

E dna comes alive at midnight.

N ight goes and day comes.

Morgan McCrimmon (9)
John Paul II Primary School, Glasgow

Colourful Autumn

On the first day of autumn,

The leaves are green on trees.

Whether the trees are big or small,

Tall or short, wide or thin,

Whether in garden or woods,

In autumn their green colour changes into different colours.

On one tree the top can be yellow,

The centre can be brown

The bottom can be red.

After autumn, there will be no leaves on trees as winter is coming.

David Mundemba (8)
John Paul II Primary School, Glasgow

Hallowe'en

H appy kids playing games and tricks
A ll the adults giving treats and nice sweets
L ovely costumes and scary ones too
L ittle children saying peekaboo!
O range pumpkin lanterns and
W ee chocolate lollipops, maybe candy
E veryone trick or treating having fun
E ating, munching, crunching and chewing
N ow everyone is trying to get to sleep, happy Hallowe'en.

Monique Petrie (10)
John Paul II Primary School, Glasgow

Autumn Is Here At Last

Autumn is here at last,
Summer went by so fast.
Crunch, crunch from the leaves,
The smell of autumn in the breeze.
All the colours golden and bright
I think I'll wear my scarf tonight.
I love the warm autumn glow,
Sometimes I wish it would never go.

Jody Taggart (10)
John Paul II Primary School, Glasgow

Untitled

Swimming pools and diving suits
Shorts and the sound of ice cream van toots
I thought it was cold
But it's really hot
Kids rolling and jumping
Jumping and bumping to find the seashells.

Scott Ramsay (7)
John Paul II Primary School, Glasgow

Hallowe'en

H allowe'en, Hallowe'en, so scared
A nd everyone laughing now
L onely dark nights
L ight some candles tonight
O ld white ghosts flying
W itches laughing
E verybody running up and down
E very monster laughing
N ow.

Christopher O'Donnell (10)
John Paul II Primary School, Glasgow

Hallowe'en Nights

Hallowe'en comes.
Hallowe'en stays.
Hallowe'en is the best.
Hallowe'en means dressing up.
Hallowe'en means lights and pumpkins in the night.
Hallowe'en means laughing and joking.
Hallowe'en means trick or treating.
Hallowe'en means treats and sweets.
Hallowe'en goes back to sleep.

Megan Hardie (8)
John Paul II Primary School, Glasgow

Autumn

I don't like this time of year.
The season is autumn and winter is near.
It gets cold, dark and very wet.
I think I will put my wellies on and then I'm set.
I'm going to stay at my gran's tonight
Because my house has no lights.

Chelsea-Lee Moody (7)
John Paul II Primary School, Glasgow

Hallowe'en

Hallowe'en is a scary night.
Giving adults such a fright.
To see a ghostie at their door,
Makes them fall down to the floor.

Apples, nuts, pumpkins, candy,
Fancy costumes look just dandy.
Little goblins, vampires, devils,
Trick or treating for their thrills.

So get together in a crowd.
Make a noise, make it loud.
Fill your bag and get home quick.
Eat all your goodies and be sick!

Alex Carson (8)
John Paul II Primary School, Glasgow

Autumn

A ll the leaves fall off the trees.
U nder the tree there is a bunch of leaves.
T rees are dying, leaves are lying.
U nder the trees, mice hide.
M uch
more
scout
clubs.
N ever
forget
autumn.

Daniel Drummond (9)
John Paul II Primary School, Glasgow

Hallowe'en

On Hallowe'en night
I got a fright
With all the bats
And big black cats.

I caught a tear
With all the fear
But it was fun
When the party had begun.

Ghosts and ghouls
Haunt the schools
And I was in stitches
When I saw all the witches
Flying past the pitches.

Darcy McBride (9)
John Paul II Primary School, Glasgow

October Birthday

October, October is the month
The fifth day of the month.
Born in 1998
So make a big cake.

1998

Birthdays come and birthdays go.
So as you know, your bones will grow.
Your bones will get stronger.
I wish I were 5 years older.
And 5-foot taller.

Dylan Griffin (9)
John Paul II Primary School, Glasgow

Hallowe'en

H allowe'en is great and fun
A nd it is not even done.
L ittle spiders grow so big and they crawl
L ong to wait until it starts.
O n Hallowe'en everyone can scream
W e are going to get so much
E vening, night, you will get a fright.
E veryone can have so much fun.
N ow we have seen enough today, we can shout hip hop hooray!

Dylan McAuley (10)
John Paul II Primary School, Glasgow

Hallowe'en

Hallowe'en is coming
Hallowe'en is here.
Hallowe'en is a scary time of year.
Boys and girls going out trick or treating.
And coming home with lots of treats.
I really like Hallowe'en
Because I get lots of sweets.

Charles Ball (9)
John Paul II Primary School, Glasgow

It's Autumn Time

A ll the leaves are changing
U nder the autumn sun
T umbling to the ground they fall
U nder our feet they crunch
M any children kicking the leaves around
N ippy, cold weather.

Abbie Morton (8)
John Paul II Primary School, Glasgow

Hallowe'en

H allowe'en, Hallowe'en.
A pples and treats.
L ollipops just for you.
L ots of fun and laughter too.
O ut and about to get some treats.
W itches and vampires out to get you.
E verybody is out to scare people.
E vil masks and scary costumes
N obody wants to miss the treats.

Nicole Boag (9)
John Paul II Primary School, Glasgow

Oh Hallowe'en! Oh Hallowe'en!

Oh Hallowe'en! Oh Hallowe'en!
It's great
I like to trick or treat until it gets late.
You get lots of nuts and sweets.
In fact, in my bag I get lots of treats.
Hallowe'en is so much fun.
Not just for me, for everyone.

Caitlyn Tervit (8)
John Paul II Primary School, Glasgow

Hallowe'en

Tall, skinny wizard laughing,
White glowing ghosts in the dark,
Scary skeletons jiggling,
Flying bats everywhere.
Ugly green witches cackling,
Big round cauldron bubbling,
Nasty spells put into the pot.
Horrible, black cat scratching,
It's Hallowe'en night!

David McKenna (11)
John Paul II Primary School, Glasgow

Hallowe'en

H orrible night to have a fright
A fter 12 look after yourself
L ate at night the ghosts are in sight.
L ook out! Look out! You will get a fright
O ver the rooftops and amongst the trees.
W itches flying with the breeze.
E very night this time of year
E vil spirits will appear
N ever forget it's Hallowe'en and keep together as a team . . . or else.

Rachel Birney (9)
John Paul II Primary School, Glasgow

Hallowe'en

H appy Hallowe'en to everyone out there
A spooky time, watch out 'cause you'll get a fright
L aughing your head off, actually, it might get chopped off
L ook out, there might be ghosts about
O h my gosh, I heard a witch cackling
W hen you're out at night you'll be out of sight
E vil creatures are about so you'll scream and shout
E nd of the night you might be missing
N ever go out on Hallowe'en again!

Lauren Donaghue (11)
John Paul II Primary School, Glasgow

Hallowe'en

Hallowe'en is very fun.
Hallowe'en is for everyone.
So come around and get some sweets.
But you will have to trick or treat.

Marcus Richford (10)
John Paul II Primary School, Glasgow

Young Writers - Little Laureates Scotland

Oh Hallowe'en

Oh Hallowe'en, oh Hallowe'en, oh Hallowe'en is fun,
Some people say it's ending, but it's only just begun.
Ghosts and ghouls and screams in the night,
Will give little children a horrible fright.

Some children dress up as cute sweet things,
Others are frightening and scary, 'oh jings',
I am dressed up as a scarecrow with big smelly feet,
And I am going round doors for a trick or treat.

It's dark and it's late and I have nice things to eat,
Off goes my hat and my big smelly feet.
I'm going home now, I'm going to run,
Oh Hallowe'en, oh Hallowe'en, oh Hallowe'en is fun . . .

Meghan Miller (9)
John Paul II Primary School, Glasgow

Hallowe'en

H umbling scary white ghosts
A red-hot devil is here to torture,
L ong white bearded wizards
L imping white skeletons,
O wls howling in the dark, dusky trees,
W itches that are ugly, green, stirring in their cauldron
E vil red-eyed black bat,
E very year it gets scarier!
N ever go out trick or treating again!

Stephen Johnston (11)
John Paul II Primary School, Glasgow

Hallowe'en

H allowe'en is finally here.
A nd all the children will appear.
L aughing and joking, it's the best.
L ook at the bats out of their nest.
O utside doing trick or treat.
W hy not take a nice sweet.
E ven though everybody is out.
E verybody, it's time to scream and shout.
N ow we can dress up and scare everybody that's about.

Sean Laverty (9)
John Paul II Primary School, Glasgow

Hallowe'en

H appy Hallowe'en to you
A ll the children say
L et's dress up and go out
L ots of sweets!
O n the wall is decoration
W e are really scared
E ating all night
E veryone sleepy
N ever forget Hallowe'en.

Lauren Kelly (10)
John Paul II Primary School, Glasgow

Zap!

Lances of lightning thundering down,
scarring trees that are perfectly brown.
Heaters in houses bringing some heat,
to those who have very cold feet.

Scott Robertson (10)
Knightswood Primary School, Glasgow

The Lightning Flash

Luminous lightning flashing through the sky
Up above so high, makes me want to cry.
Scary street lights flashing on and off.
A burning toaster makes me cough.
Make sure you turn all the lamps off at night
Or you might wake up and have a fright.

Millar Hendry (10)
Knightswood Primary School, Glasgow

Electricity

Electricity is everywhere,
Wonky wires over there.
Baldy bulbs in a lamp,
Never touch anything if your hands are damp.
Clever circuits here and there
Electricity.

Amy Wilson (10)
Knightswood Primary School, Glasgow

Zapz!

Electrons are everywhere
Don't repair them without a care
Or maybe you'll get a zap
Then you'll go for a really big nap
Batteries used all the time
I hope you liked Zappy Rhyme.

Luke McGunnigle (10)
Knightswood Primary School, Glasgow

If I Could Touch The Sky

If I could touch the sky
I would touch a butterfly
And ride it to my house
And then keep it for a pet.

If I could touch the sky
I would grab a butterfly
And keep it for my best friend
And play with him in the garden.

Amy Hopkins (7)
Knightswood Primary School, Glasgow

If I Could Touch The Sky

If I could touch the sky
I would grab an angel
And put it in my room
Then I would let it go.

If I could touch the sky
I would catch a bird
And use it as my pet.

Lauren Doran (6)
Knightswood Primary School, Glasgow

If I Could Touch The Sky

If I could touch the sky
I would pull down a butterfly
And use it for my teddy.

If I could touch the sky
I would grab a plane
And use it for my dolls.

Kara Patrick (7)
Knightswood Primary School, Glasgow

If I Could Touch The Sky

If I could touch the sky
I would go to the moon
And use it as a football.

If I could touch the sky
I would pull a star
And use it for a lamp.

Josh Lawson
Knightswood Primary School, Glasgow

If I Could Touch The Sky

If I could touch the sky
I would grab a star
And hang it up in my room.

If I could touch the sky
I would grab a moon
And give it to my brother.

Ryan Gardner (7)
Knightswood Primary School, Glasgow

If I Could Touch The Sky

If I could touch the sky
I would grab a butterfly
And I would use it for my pet and feed it.

If I could touch the sky
I would reach a star
And give it to my friends.

Leah McGunnigle (6)
Knightswood Primary School, Glasgow

If I Could Touch The Sky

If I could touch the sky
I would grab a star
And give it to the poor.

If I could touch the sky
I would grab a butterfly
And put it in my hair.

Megan Tolland (7)
Knightswood Primary School, Glasgow

If I Could Touch The Sky

If I could touch the sky
I would grab an angel and use it
For my doll and then let it go.

If I could touch the sky
I would pull down a rainbow
And use it for my banana bed.

Courtney Johnston (7)
Knightswood Primary School, Glasgow

If I Could Touch The Sky

If I could touch the sky
I would grab a star and make wishes
And wish that I were rich.

If I could touch the sky
I would catch a rainbow
And use it for a light.

Russell McGill (7)
Knightswood Primary School, Glasgow

If I Could Touch The Sky

If I could touch the sky
I would grab a bird and take it home for my mum as a present
And I would grab a rainbow and moon for my bedroom.

If I could touch the sky
I would catch a butterfly
And give it a home.

Megan Houghton (7)
Knightswood Primary School, Glasgow

If I Could Touch The Sky

If I could touch the sky
I would grab a cloud for my pillow.

If I could touch the sky
I would grab a rainbow for my bedroom
I would grab an angel too.

Jade Doyle (6)
Knightswood Primary School, Glasgow

If I Could Touch The Sky

If I could touch the sky
I would grab a plane and play with it.

If I could touch the sky
I would grab a helicopter and play with it.

Michael Fitzpatrick (5)
Knightswood Primary School, Glasgow

If I Could Touch The Sky

If I could touch the sky
I would catch a star and I would put it in my bedroom.

If I could touch the sky
I would catch a plane and it would take me on a holiday
And I would go to the beach and build a sandcastle.

Connor Doogan
Knightswood Primary School, Glasgow

Electricity

Electricity is everywhere,
Even if you have short hair.
Electricity high and low,
Powers through the rain and snow.
Super sockets in the house,
Can kill even a little mouse.
Brave batteries in some cool toys,
Is the safest electrical for girls and boys.
Electricity is everywhere
So everybody be aware!

Lauren Patrick (10)
Knightswood Primary School, Glasgow

If I Could Touch The Sky

If I could touch the sky
I would pull an angel down and use it to be my pet.

If I could touch the sky
I would grab a star and use it for my pillow.

Emma Quinn
Knightswood Primary School, Glasgow

Bulbs

If you touch them when they're on,
You could die if watching King Kong.
Turn them off before you go out,
It really is your shout!
They could even start a fire,
Or you could trip on an electric wire!
This is why you should not do it,
After all you don't want to lose it!

Lesley Coia (10)
Knightswood Primary School, Glasgow

Electric Bolt

Electric, electric, it's everywhere,
It's upstairs, downstairs, it's everywhere.
Bright, bright lights in your bathroom
But if they fall in the tub you'll be dead in a sec
So don't take the risk
Wet fingers near switches, baby fingers near sockets.
Crazy kites near power lines, it's a bad place to fly,
And if that kite hits the power line you're dead in a flash!

Lewis Harrison (10)
Knightswood Primary School, Glasgow

Laser Light

Electricity is everywhere,
Heating heaters here and there.
Don't touch sockets with wet hands,
Or you'll be dead in a flash!
Making circuits is so fun,
Lighting bulbs with everyone.
So be careful around the house,
Or you'll be dead like a mouse!

Leena Gurung (10)
Knightswood Primary School, Glasgow

My Cat

My cat.
Sat in a hat.
Of course he is not fat.
So I gave him a pat just for that.

He likes his meat.
But one day it was too sweet,
Because of the heat.
On his seat.

He done a poo.
In my dad's shoe.
While he was in the loo.
Doing a number two.

He heard it flush.
Then he blushed.
Then he rushed.
So hush.

He ran.
Into a frying pan.
And he got a tan.
Now you know my cat Stan.

Chantel Fraser (11)
Knightswood Primary School, Glasgow

If I Could Touch The Sky

If I could touch the sky
I would grab a rainbow
And use it for a slide.

If I could touch the sky
I would grab a butterfly
So I could fly.

Annalise Gillan
Knightswood Primary School, Glasgow

If I Could Touch The Sky

If I could touch the sky
I would grab a moon and use it as my football
On the field and score a goal
And my dad might play with me.

If I could touch the sky
I would catch a cloud and use it for my pillow
And it would be comfy.

Paul Cairns
Knightswood Primary School, Glasgow

Super Bolt

Electric lighting socket,
Don't you touch it or you will fly like a rocket!
If you do you will end up like stew
And that will be the end of you.

Sean Miller (10)
Knightswood Primary School, Glasgow

Fear

Fear is black like crows covering the sky
It looks like a dark house at night
It sounds like bears howling in the distance
It smells like a rubbish dump in the middle of nowhere
It feels like the blade of a knife
It tastes like a dead hairy tarantula
It reminds me of being surrounded by beetles.

Kyle Rodger (8)
Langbank Primary School, Langbank

The People In My Head

When I go to bed at night and fall straight to sleep
The people in my head wake and start to creep
First they run around my head
Then from there they slide down my leg
After that they bounce on my heart
Next they run through my ribs and start to dart

In and out is a game they play
Hooray is what I think they say
Left out right, here, there
Running about, it is not fair
In the morning when I awake
From head to toe my body aches
Oh I wish they would not wake
So I can sleep well! For goodness sake!

Jennifer Hemphill (11)
Langbank Primary School, Langbank

Dragon Of The Night

Goliath the dragon comes out at night
He is long and wide, he might give you a fright
But don't be alarmed, he will not bite
For he is friendly, he does not fight

He is nice and sweet if you treat him well
I am sure he likes you, can you not tell?
Swiftly and safely he will give you a ride
Perhaps down to the beach along by the tide

He likes to slide in the sand and swim in the sea
Being out in the night makes him feel so free
When the sun comes up he will be in his caves
Snoring and sleeping soundly by the waves.

Ross Tyre (8)
Langbank Primary School, Langbank

Happiness

Happiness is green like grass on a warm summer's day
It sounds like children singing Christmas carols
It smells like hot melted chocolate
It feels like a soft rug that is brand new
It tastes like creamy coffee
It looks like someone scoring a hat-trick
It reminds me of my birthday in school.

Gavin Hemphill (8)
Langbank Primary School, Langbank

Anger

Anger is dark red like a fire in the forest
It looks like a volcano erupting
It tastes like hot chillies
It smells like rotten dead fish
It feels like a spiky cactus
It sounds like steam coming out a kettle
It reminds me of teeth crunching.

Eve Lapping (9)
Langbank Primary School, Langbank

Swapping And Sharing

Shopping, shopping, shopping every single day,
Shopping, shopping, shopping, who will I get today?
I love to buy my Dr Who cards and swap them with my friends
Who will have this? Will I get that?
'Put those away,' my teacher yells
But under the desks we continue to swap
As it's too important to stop!

Jason Gallacher (9)
Our Holy Redeemer's Primary School, Clydebank

Football

Before the football began we shook hands for a good game.
The game started when I kicked off and my boot fell off!
I tied my lace and started running with a pace.
I was so desperate to win so I scored a goal
And led my team to victory!

Dario Cocozza (9)
Our Holy Redeemer's Primary School, Clydebank

The Sun

The sun is bright and sparkly
And it sparkles in my face
So every time it says goodbye
I think I have to cry

The sun is a star that is yellow and orange
With a smile on its face
It comes to Earth at daytime
And goes home at night-time
So the moon comes out at night-time
I love the sun.

Sarah Brown (9)
Our Holy Redeemer's Primary School, Clydebank

Christmas

People singing carols.
Bells ringing all day.
When it is only Christmas Eve.
Hip hip hip hooray.
It is lifetime this Christmas,
Guessing what I'm going to get.
Hoping that my presents are the best ones ever yet.

Morgan Bell (9)
Our Holy Redeemer's Primary School, Clydebank

My Bad Moments

I loved to visit my great Granda,
Who always had a smile.
When it came to Christmas,
I was so delighted.
But when I heard the bad news,
I was very, very sad.
Although I had to move on,
I never spoke of him again.

Ross Ferrier (9)
Our Holy Redeemer's Primary School, Clydebank

Toy Cars

You can make them fly,
You can make them break,
I often wonder if they are easy to make.
You can make them go fast and do a big skid,
They even make my dad act like a big kid,
It's definitely better to play with cars than sit around eating Mars bars.

Frankie Burns (9)
Our Holy Redeemer's Primary School, Clydebank

Shop

I like to shop until I pop,
Shoes, bags, I never wear rags.
I wear spotted skirts, never dotted skirts.
I like shirts that are pink, they always make me wink.
Shoes that shine are always mine,
I wear trousers when it's colder,
It is as cold as a boulder nowadays
But I still go out to play my way.

Courtney Gallagher (9)
Our Holy Redeemer's Primary School, Clydebank

Hallowe'en

Hallowe'en, Hallowe'en.
Ghosts and witches to be seen.
Ghosts, ghosts gathered round, eating toast which they found.
Decorations everywhere witches flying in the air.
Trick or treat, trick or treat, ghouls coming up your street.
Children wearing fancy clothes, going around knocking on doors.

Stephen Cullen (9)
Our Holy Redeemer's Primary School, Clydebank

Football

Football is fun, much better than a gun.
Rugby is cool, but not as good as football.
In comes a ball that will fall in my goal.
But a ball bursts in the air, on my head,
And on the ground as well.
And everyone is football crazy, football mad.
But as the ball bursts we can't play.
And we go home with heavy hearts.

Darren Dolan (9)
Our Holy Redeemer's Primary School, Clydebank

Waterfall

You see the light blue water,
Falling from the waterfall.
It hits the rocks at the bottom
And knocks the shabby brown walls.

I like to hear the water booming off the ground.
Every time the water splashes, it goes in my eyes.

Anthony Smith (9)
Our Holy Redeemer's Primary School, Clydebank

The Litter Bug And The Normal Boy

There once was a little bug,
He put litter everywhere,
He put it in the park,
He put it in his school.
He even put it in his class!

Then one day a normal boy came by,
He knew what he had to do.
He picked the litter up and put it in the bin.
As I watched that boy it was plain for me to see,
That I would rather be like that boy than the litter bug I used to be!

Aaron Keenan (9)
Our Holy Redeemer's Primary School, Clydebank

My Dog Is A Friend

Monty is my favourite dog!
I mostly take him to school
He sits on my desk for a while
And always makes me smile!

I also have another dog
He is proud of his lovely brown collar
But I am sure he would love to be taller!
He's got big strong ears that flop in the air
And I love to spend time brushing his hair.
With a brown dry nose and deep shiny black eyes
From his ragged mouth he releases a sigh
As I am sure he would love to be Monty.

Johanna Doyle (9)
Our Holy Redeemer's Primary School, Clydebank

Stuff And Nonsense

Stuff and nonsense here and there,
But when I think there's nothing to do
Something always comes out of the blue.

I wish it would all stop!
If I am not asked to paint a door,
I am asked to walk a dog.
I am sick of getting asked to do something
I wish I could just sit back on a cosy soft chair and watch TV all day.

Shannon Davidson (9)
Our Holy Redeemer's Primary School, Clydebank

My Gran

My gran died,
She was really important to me.
I really miss her,
And I wish she was here right now.
I love her so much,
I want to cry.
I can remember all the things she got me,
And all the important things she did for me
I want her to come alive again,
But then she will die again.

Shelby McGuiness (9)
Our Holy Redeemer's Primary School, Clydebank

The Black Night

Have you seen the Black Knight
Escaping the flaming tower?

Have you seen the Black Knight
Heaving his heavy armour?

Have you seen the Black Knight
Slaying the fiery dragon?

Luke Stewart (9)
Overton Primary School, Greenock

My Baby Cousin

My baby cousin is the cutest boy on Earth
He is so lovely; I'd like to visit him in Perth.

When I lay him in his cot
I think he's sleeping . . . but he's not.

When I smell him he smells like a rose
But not until I smell his toes!

My baby cousin is the cutest boy ever
I love him so much, I'll love him forever.

Cheyenne Adamson (10)
Overton Primary School, Greenock

My Comfy Bed

I go to bed and rest my head
All warm and cosy, I love to lie!
When I look up at the sky
I feel a bit dozy and start to cry

In the morning when I wake up
The sky is light and I sit up
I climb out of my comfy bed
And start to shake my lazy head.

James Barclay (10)
Overton Primary School, Greenock

Health

H elp eat healthy, do not waste.
E nterprising healthy tuck shop.
A pples, grapes, great things to eat.
L emons too are good for you.
T asting all different kinds of fruit.
H elping raise money for the school.
Y ou eat fruit to be healthy.

Kristy McGunnigle (8)
Overton Primary School, Greenock

My Choir

My choir, my choir, my beautiful choir
C is for children singing at the same time.
My choir, my choir, my lovely choir
H is for how well we sing together.
My choir, my choir, my talented choir.
O is for 'oh' the beautiful sound.
My choir, my choir, my musical choir.
I is for ink for the words in the song.
My choir, my choir, my wonderful choir.
R is for reaching all the notes.
My choir, my choir, my excellent choir.

Gemma Ferguson (9)
Overton Primary School, Greenock

My Great Grandad

My great grandad was so sweet
I didn't want him to die
He used to be in a hospital
Then the machine went *beeeeeeeeeep!*

I really loved him
Things will never be the same
I just really loved him
I have no one to blame

My great granny misses him
So do the rest
When I heard it I felt really dim
But he's simply the best

I know he's taking care of me
When I look up at the sky
All that I can see
Is my great grandad looking down on me.

Aidan Conway (10)
Overton Primary School, Greenock

Anger

Anger is vicious like a fierce growling dog
It sounds like a steaming kettle going through my head
It smells like a sweaty boxer fighting
It looks like a ripping vicious tiger
It tastes like the ashes from a burning fire
It feels like the scratching of an old cat
It reminds me of the time of the bombing bomb.

Erin Edwards (8)
Overton Primary School, Greenock

British Wildlife

British wildlife everywhere
In your house, up the stairs
At the seaside, in the sky
Everywhere you look, wildlife is everywhere

Squirrel storing food for the winter
Hedgehogs going across the road
I hope they follow the green cross code!
Fox carrying a rabbit, poor little rabbit

Little raccoon in that bin
Maybe you will find a tin
Little sparrow in the sky
How do you fly up so high?

Peregrine falcon swooping down
Far away from town
Little robin with a berry
Or maybe it's a cherry?

British wildlife everywhere
You can find it everywhere.

Aidan Regan (10)
Overton Primary School, Greenock

Dogs

Dogs are my favourite animals
Especially my own dog Poppy
She is really playful and can jump really high in the sky

My other dog Bruce
He was the quietest ever
But when he passed away
It made my skin shiver
But now I know he's up in Heaven
Lying in a bright blue river

My other dog Scezza was an English pit bull
Sometimes I thought he could break a statue like a hammering tool
And he was that strong he could lift a bull!

Simba was a beggar boy
He used to always beg for his toy
He was so small he looked like a fur ball
You'd think he was in the army because he used to always crawl.

Dogs are the best animals ever!

Rhys Arlow (10)
Overton Primary School, Greenock

My Best Friend - Haiku

I have a fun friend
His name is Craig Robertson
He is just so cool.

Craig Kincaid (9)
Overton Primary School, Greenock

Class Rules

C is for watch the clock tick-tock
L is for listen and don't talk
A is for attention *stop!*
S is for sorry that is wrong
S is for sort that out now

R is for don't rub out
U is for Uranus, Neptune and Pluto
L is for look and don't look away
E is for don't break the equipment
S is for Overton Primary School.

Natalie Chan (9)
Overton Primary School, Greenock

Toys In The Toybox

A rocking horse, with hair so silky long
A ballet dancer, dancing to the pretty song
A racing car, whizzing round the metal track
A fluffy teddy bear, eating a yummy snack

Toys, toys everywhere
From a giraffe . . . to teddy bears
Toys, toys all over the place
A rag doll with a pretty face

A football, ready to score the winning goal
A wind-up mouse, darting into a hole
A toy farm, with a little white lamb
A play supermarket, filled with eggs and ham

Toys, toys in the box
From cars to a teddy fox
Toys, toys all over the floor
This is simply *toys galore!*

Sarah Hunter (10)
Overton Primary School, Greenock

Dinosaurs

Dinosaurs, dinosaurs!
All shades of colours
Brown, grey and green
Dinosaurs, dinosaurs!

Dinosaurs, dinosaurs!
Loud and eerie
Sounds like an off tune trumpet
Dinosaurs, dinosaurs!

Dinosaurs, dinosaurs!
Big and scaly
And look very scary
Dinosaurs, dinosaurs!

Dinosaurs, dinosaurs!
They give out a bad smell
They look so dirty
I've seen one, I can tell
Dinosaurs, dinosaurs!

Dylan McGunnigle (10)
Overton Primary School, Greenock

Old Things

My favourite things are old things
Like sirens that sing and magic rings.

My favourite things are dino bones
And not when my sister moans!

My favourite thing is an ammonite
If you ever see one you'll know I'm right.

But my most favourite thing is my grandad
When he passed away I felt real sad.

Evan McQuillan (10)
Overton Primary School, Greenock

Friends

Friends! Friends! Galore
If I have too many I might start to snore
Two of them called Cameron and Drew
They're simply the best, better than all the rest

We play games like football and basketball
But what I'm still looking for is my ball
But when I always go in for tea I always say
Look Mum I fell and grazed my knee

We play games like hide-and-seek
I always get got when I shout peek!
Then I got my life scared out by a sheep
Then we played rugby someone fell, then we all were in a heap

When I go for a shower then I need my dad's
Aftershave power
I had to get a plaster on and in the morning
I was such a big howler.

Lee Alexander Donald (10)
Overton Primary School, Greenock

Hallowe'en The Pumpkin King

Hallowe'en, a frightening night.
Go out if you want a fright.
Come on the pumpkin king is here!

Hallowe'en a frightening night.
You can go home if you want a bite,
Come on the pumpkin king is here!

Hallowe'en, a frightening night.
Did you frighten anyone last night?
Come on the pumpkin king is here!

Liam Hare (10)
Overton Primary School, Greenock

Popcorn!

Popcorn, popcorn everywhere!
I'm so greedy I never have any to spare!
Popcorn, popcorn only me!
I just wish it was all free!

Popcorn, popcorn oh galore!
When I'm finished I need some more!
Popcorn, popcorn oh dear!
I'm more obsessed than men with beer!

Popcorn, popcorn oh my gosh!
After eating that sticky stuff I need a wash!
Popcorn, popcorn after all!
I like eating it more than kicking a ball!

Popcorn, popcorn all over!
When I eat it all I'll need a Range Rover!
Popcorn, popcorn none left!
I guess I'll just have to turn to theft!

Popcorn, popcorn in the sea!
I always have it with my tea!
Popcorn, popcorn I've had enough!
After eating that sticky stuff!

Cameron Henry (10)
Overton Primary School, Greenock

My Special Friend - Haiku

My best friend Zoe
We stick together like glue
We're the best of pals.

Chelsi Buchan (9)
Overton Primary School, Greenock

My Cat Snuggels

I have a cat called Snuggels
And she just loves cuddles
On my bed I pat her head
I have a cat called Snuggels

I have a cat called Snuggels
She always plays with string
And is scared when the doorbell rings
I have a cat called Snuggels

I have a cat called Snuggels
She has lots of names like Juggles
And another great one like Bubbles
I have a cat called Snuggels

I have a cat called Snuggels
She is the best
Better than all the rest
I have a great cat called Snuggels.

Sean Wilkie (10)
Overton Primary School, Greenock

An Amazing Friend - Haiku

Alan, my best friend
He makes me laugh all the time,
He's always helpful.

Rhys Evans (10)
Overton Primary School, Greenock

A Good Friend - Haiku

Friends are forever
They stick together like glue
They're a part of life.

Sophie McCormick (9)
Overton Primary School, Greenock

My Great Uncle

My great uncle was the best guy in the world
Until he went to war
I cannot remember what war he was in
So I will throw that thinking cap in the bin

My uncle was among such brave men
He used to hide in the sniper's den
He did not always use a sniper
Sometimes a MP5N

When he came home he had such a cool crib
But when he went back to war he got shot in the rib
By another sniper

Lots of morphine he was given
And on his grave there was a red ribbon.

Drew Hepburn (10)
Overton Primary School, Greenock

Love

Love is the key to happiness
Love sounds like the bells in the church
Love tastes like melted chocolate and cream
Love looks like a beautiful angel from her cloud
Love smells like sweet honey that's from the bees
Love feels like a really loving family
Love reminds me of a warm feeling inside.

Caragh Jamison (9)
Overton Primary School, Greenock

Church

We go to church on a Sunday
The adults pray
And the children play

We go to church on a Sunday
We listen to speeches
And the minister teaches

We go to church on a Sunday
We sing songs
And listen to the bells going ding-dong.

Steven Donald (8)
Overton Primary School, Greenock

Happiness

Happiness is presents.
Happiness sounds like birds singing.
Happiness tastes like pasta in tomato sauce.
Happiness looks like a fluffy cloud.
Happiness smells like daffodil flowers.
Happiness feels like a soft blanket to wrap around me.
It reminds me of a snowy Christmas Day.

Rebecca Heron & Euan Hare (9)
Overton Primary School, Greenock

Hallowe'en

H aunted house
A lone in the dark
L ooking for witches
L ost in the very dark
O oooh! Hallowe'en is oh so scary!
W itches in the sky
E at lots of sweets
E verybody dressed up
N othing to me is scary tonight.

Samantha Woods
Overton Primary School, Greenock

Happiness

Happiness is silky blossoms.
Happiness sounds like cheerfulness.
Happiness tastes like rainbow-coloured ice cream.
Happiness looks like falling into a dream.
Happiness smells like my mum's washing in the morning.
Happiness feels like my mum's hot chocolate in the morning.
Happiness reminds me of waking up on Christmas morning to
dumpling.

Kyra Copeland (9)
Overton Primary School, Greenock

Happiness

Happiness is lovely on a Saturday morning and hearing the birds sing
Happiness sounds like children playing in the park on a Sunday
Happiness tastes like the chocolate melting in my mouth
Happiness looks like the rainbow shining in the sky
Happiness smells like roses from the freshest garden
Happiness feels like the fire warming me up
It reminds me of ice cream and a box of chocolates.

Kayleigh Turner (9)
Overton Primary School, Greenock

Scooby-Doo

S is for Scooby snack, he shoves them in his mouth.
C is for catch the ghost, he gets them every time.
O is for the octopus monster, I thought he'd never get away.
O is for oh no a monster is chasing him again.
B is for best friend Shaggy - he's funny and good.
Y is for yikes! It's Shaggy's favourite word.

D is for Daphne. She's funny and smart too.
O is the original show, it's better than the movie.
O is for ooh goes Scooby-Doo when he sees a monster.

Ryan Harper (9)
Overton Primary School, Greenock

The Birds

The birds sing when you're asleep
Sometimes have a peep
Through your colourful
Bedroom window
They don't mind when you give them food
But only when you could
To keep them fit, healthy and great.

Chloe Munro (9)
Overton Primary School, Greenock

Fear

Fear is something you are so scared of and you will not fight back
Fear sounds like the screaming of a terrified baby in her cot
Fear tastes like the gurgling in my shaky mouth
Fear looks like the darkness of tears
Fear smells like the sweat of your body
Fear feels like you're getting attacked by a tiger
It reminds me of a person crying when they're scared.

Megan Ruddy (9)
Overton Primary School, Greenock

Spelling

S ilent letters - difficult to spell.
P atterns in words help us work them out.
E xtra and extension in my spelling book.
L anguage makes sense when spelt correctly.
L earn about complicated words and sounds.
I nky stamps on our pages.
N ever forget to do your spelling homework
G ood work deserves a plus.

Megan Felgate (9)
Overton Primary School, Greenock

Anger

Anger is grey like the gloomy sky above.
It sounds like someone shouting from the heavens beyond.
It smells like the fire that will never shed its flames.
It looks like an explosion from your head out of your angry mouth.
It tastes like the cursed fish that is covered in horrible gloopy slime.
It feels like the scratching of nails going down the blackboard
That echoes through my body.
It reminds me of the loud vast lion that pounces in the dark night.

Annabel Black (9)
Overton Primary School, Greenock

Love

Love is being with my mum every day
Love sounds like the way my mum talks to me
Love tastes like the toast my mum makes me in the morning
Love looks like me and my mum in all the pictures that we are in
Love feels like the bedtime kiss my mum gives me at night
Love reminds me of the day I was born and seeing my mum's
Face for the first time.

Cara Cunningham (9)
Overton Primary School, Greenock

Hero Legend

I am a hero
I have the speed of a cheetah
and the power of a lion.
I have slayed a dragon
Climbed very big mountains.
Now I am a legend.

I have a great adventure
but my name is lost in time.
Though I know that I can have
those dreams of that great adventure.

Harry Mackie (11)
Richmond Park School, Glasgow

Football

F ootball, football
O ver the line
O fficial blows his whistle
T urned away by the keeper
B all hits the camera
A sk the ref why it was a yellow card
L anded awkwardly
L ashing down with rain.

Michael Love (11)
Richmond Park School, Glasgow

Cinemas

C inemas are good
I nside only
N ice and quiet
E very weekend I go
M ustn't shout
A mazing.

Kieran Boult (11)
Richmond Park School, Glasgow

I Love

I love:
Bright sun
Night
Tea
Toast
My name
Toys
Boys
Violence
School
People
Weddings
And my brothers and sisters
And my mum and dad
Holidays
Grandparents
And lots and lots of ice cream.

Gemma McGowan (10)
Richmond Park School, Glasgow

Snooker

Snooker is the best
and all the players
must pot balls if
they want to win.

They must hit the
cue ball inch perfect
if they want to pot
the ball in.

Ramzan Akram (10)
Richmond Park School, Glasgow

Super Crimes

I am a super cop.
I use:
Utility belt
Cape
Bullet-proof vest
Cuffs
Armoured truck
Machine gun
Hand gun
Baton
High-tech boots
Fireproof trousers
Fireproof helmet
Night vision goggles

I have many powers and equipment.
I am very strong.
I stop crimes all over the town.
I was walking down the street when suddenly
I bumped into a man with a gun.
I stopped him.
I arrested him and took him to the police station
I threw him in jail.

Gerard McQuade (11)
Richmond Park School, Glasgow

Hallowe'en

All the schools are filled with ghouls.
And there are bats and cats everywhere.
As all the witches' noses twitch,
The ghost is eating toast,
A witch's broom is going vroom
High in the sky.

Charlotte Reilly (9)
St Agnes' Primary School, Glasgow

The Dentist

Oh, I hate the dentist,
I don't like it one bit.
But when I go,
I always know my teeth are looking fit.

I hate it when he uses the thing,
That taps and taps my teeth.
I hate it when he uses the gas,
That smells like mum's corned beef.

But when it's over, done and dusted,
I say to the dentist you've been trusted
To clean my teeth as well as you can,
And not give me teeth like a wee old man.

Anna Shields (11)
St Agnes' Primary School, Glasgow

Around The World

They all say a guy went around the world in 80 days.
I bet there were 12 different ways
Next day on a boat trip crossed 5 bays
On a jet ski with my pal Billy we heard sounds
My pal said they're coming from underground
I said don't be silly Billy!

Sophy McAloon (8)
St Agnes' Primary School, Glasgow

Rainbows

Rainbow, rainbow in the sky
Rainbow, rainbow in July
Rainbow, rainbow don't be shy
Rainbow in the sky
Rainbow in July
Rainbow don't be shy.

Tasha Gilmartin (8)
St Agnes' Primary School, Glasgow

The Terrible Fright

I got my hair weaved at night.
It was all right.
I went to bed late at night.
When I woke up in the morning
I got such a terrible fright
I got a cold, cold shiver
'Cause when I looked in the mirror
That's when I got the cold, cold shiver.

Shannon Hamilton (9)
St Agnes' Primary School, Glasgow

The Love . . .

The *boom!* of love coming out from my heart.
The caramel chocolate swirling through my mouth,
It goes up and up with love.

                    The peace and quiet throughout the day
                    Makes my stomach rumble with love . . .

I bless myself from loving
And not being cold anymore.

Caitlin Fitzpatrick (11)
St Cadoc's Primary School, Newton Mearns

Darkness

D is for darkness which is always here at night
A is for angry people always trying to fight
R is for the raging of the drunk passers-by
K is for the kicking of the gangs in fights at night
N is for the noise of the dogs howling constantly
E is for the evil people wandering around at night
S is for the syringes being left out until the morning
S is for the sound of the drunk people singing.

Ewan Forsyth (11)
St Cadoc's Primary School, Newton Mearns

Love

Love sounds like my heart that beats for you,
It sounds like the wind with a sway and a swoosh,
It sounds like the white doves singing for me,
Knowing it's a message from you makes me love you more than I do.

Love tastes like honey as sweet as you are,
It tastes like the chocolate I send you with all of my heart,
It tastes like Heaven above knowing nothing can take us apart.

Love feels like the time I met you knowing I still love you as I still do,
It feels like the time you had to go home dreading
And knowing soon I would be alone,
It feels like the time you told me I love you
And in return I told you I do too.

Love tastes like the smell of your sweet perfume,
It smells like each time I met you knowing my heart smells like fume,
It smells like the love I give to you.

Love looks like the beauty of your eyes,
It looks like the times I give you a surprise,
It looks like the beauty of life knowing with you I need to be precious.

Isla Nosratzadeh (10)
St Cadoc's Primary School, Newton Mearns

Love Is A Dream

Love is a mystery,
Is it round or square or is it a triangle?
One thing I know it is deep!
There is something we are all not sure of, does it exist?
What does it taste like?
Candy or cake?
What does it smell like?
Hot cocoa on a rainy day?

How does it feel?
Like you complete yourself for that first time.
It sounds like Romeo and Juliet.

Brogan Bennett (11)
St Cadoc's Primary School, Newton Mearns

The Entity

It rises from the mind, it hides within the brain,
I try to stop it taking over, I try and try in vain.
Too late, it's won, I failed the test, now my hair is standing on end,
I'm terrified, what should I do? Is there someone hiding
Round the bend?

It turns my sweetest merry dreams,
Into nightmares full of shouts and screams.
It wakes me up in the middle of the night,
It always wins the hardest fight.

I cry and cry until it stops,
I run before it hits the tops.
It sends freaky chills through my spine,
Then suddenly I feel fine.

This crazy thing is very scary,
Things can get extremely hairy.
This is a thing you can feel and hear,
Okay you guessed it, the mysterious entity is *fear!*

Christopher McNulty (10)
St Cadoc's Primary School, Newton Mearns

Without Any Light

Darkness sounds like your worst fears all around.
Darkness tastes so bitter like a freezer in your mouth,
Like a foul blue cheese crumbling in your teeth.
Darkness smells like rotten fish one hundred days old,
Like corpses buried not far from high ground.
Darkness looks like an empty sky,
Like there's nothing way up high.
Darkness feels like an empty field,
Like a mountain with no rocks.
Darkness reminds me of when I'm sleeping,
So all in all it's not so scary.

Liam King (10)
St Cadoc's Primary School, Newton Mearns

Hungry Children

Here I am sitting in the street,
I watch as the people pass me in a fleet.
Rumble, rumble, it feels so funny,
Rumble, rumble, it's my tummy.
I have no home,
I have no money,
But I need some cos it hurts my tummy.
I put out my hand and start to sing,
After two hours it starts to sting.
I begin to cry, shout and weep,
Please give me some food,
I don't care if it's cheap,
I don't care if it's thick,
I don't care if it's thin,
I don't even care if it comes from the bin!
Then something round was thrust in my hand,
I looked up, it was from a man,
'Here is £2, go get some food
I promise it will make you feel very good.'

Joe Devine (11)
St Cadoc's Primary School, Newton Mearns

The Laughing Picnic

Running and jumping in the sun
Is where all the laughter had begun.

We went to the park and smelt ice cream,
All our favourite flavours, it was a dream.

We had a water fight and got soaked right down
And we looked like very funny clowns.

We laughed and laughed the rest of the day
Sniggering and giggling then we had more play.

Playing and eating was the best part
Of our laughing picnic that day at the park.

Sara Stevenson (11)
St Cadoc's Primary School, Newton Mearns

At The Carnival

I walked in the gates at the front door.
Noise in my head and vibrating on the floor!
As I ran forward, the wind in my face,
I ran to my favourite, the amusement place.
I went to do a lucky dip,
And won a teddy called Mr Pip.
I then walked over to the little zoo,
And saw a monkey and a kangaroo!
Then I saw a rollercoaster orange and blue,
I watched it go then I joined the queue.
I was in the carriage up the hill.
Beginning to feel a little ill,
I felt weird, I couldn't look,
Suddenly I had to puke!
I got off the ride and into the car,
I never went back, it was a ride too far!

Hannah Duffy (11)
St Cadoc's Primary School, Newton Mearns

The Old Lady

I am going to the adventure,
My mum said, 'Be back by dark.'
I saw an old lady,
She said, 'I am Brady,
That's me,
That's what they call me.'
I said, 'Would you like a cup of tea?'
'That would be lovely.'
I took her to my house.
She saw a little mouse.
I said, 'It's OK!'
But she had all ready run away.

Ryan Higgins (10)
St Cadoc's Primary School, Newton Mearns

Fun Excuses

'I said to be in at six.'
'We were making a den with sticks.'
'Why weren't you home at seven?'
'I was playing with the yo-yo I'd been given.'
'What were you doing at eight?'
'At pottery class making this plate.'
'So where were you at nine?'
'I didn't have the time.'
'Why couldn't you make it for ten?'
'Back to fix the den.'
'I was waiting for you at eleven.'
'Sorry, remember what I was doing at seven.'
'I was here at twelve.'
'Helping Dad fix the shelf.'
'Surely you could have been here at one.'
'I was playing cowboys with my toy gun.'
'Why not two?'
'I was at Pete's sewing my ripped shoe.'
'And what about three?'
'I was away up in the old oak tree.'
'How about four?'
'I couldn't make it as my bike tyre tore.'
'Have you got anything against five?'
'Ermm . . .'
'Shhh! You think that life is a skive.'
'None of these are lies I swear, not one.'
'I suppose all you want is some fun.'

James Duncan (11)
St Cadoc's Primary School, Newton Mearns

Light And Darkness

Pin drop silence is what the darkness sounds like.
Loud and cheerful is what the light sounds like.

Darkness is evil, stealthy and repulsive,
It's like your worst nightmare come alive!

Light is friendly, proud and beautiful,
It's a lovely dream that's come into your life.

Darkness tastes like rotten fish,
Like filthy, horrible, rotten fish!

Light tastes like a chocolate fountain,
Like a lovely, mouth-watering chocolate fountain.

Darkness smells like a foul scent.
Light smells of scented perfume.

Darkness is sinister, dark and towering.
Darkness is like the end of the world.

Light is light, bright and joyful.
Light is your friend all the way to the end.

Darkness feels like gloopy sour milk!
Light feels like precious silk.

Dark and light.

John Connor (10)
St Cadoc's Primary School, Newton Mearns

Darkness

Darkness, darkness,
Sounds like the roar of wind
Or screaming of the thunder.

Darkness, darkness,
Scared or fine,
I can see something that is not mine.

Darkness, darkness,
Heart beating fast
In the black of night.

Darkness, darkness,
I feel as if I will never see the light.

Darkness, darkness,
I close my eyes,
Suddenly I see lots of lies.

Darkness, darkness,
Tastes like blood
From falling in the mud.

Nicola Ormiston (11)
St Cadoc's Primary School, Newton Mearns

Puppy Luv

I have a puppy
And her name is Lucky.
She's always with me at night
Or even when I get a fright.
She's made of sugar 'n' spice
And everything nice.

When I take her to play
We both shout 'Hooray!'
Then her friends meet with her
And that's a real treat for her.
But when we go home
I know I'm not alone.
When I go to bed
I start to say I had a great day.
Lucky comes to bed with me
And I'm starting to get dreamy.
I loved my day, it was definitely not grey,
I had tons of fun in the sun.

My day can never get better
With my lovely duvely puppy . . . *Lucky!*

Laura Connelly (10)
St Cadoc's Primary School, Newton Mearns

Fun In The Sun

As I go to the play area I see my friend having her tea.
My friend and I walk together, friends forever.
We meet another friend, which makes us three.
We'll stay with each other, and yet it will always be.
As we reach the play area we go to play.
We get really hungry, so we buy lots of sweets and treats.
Then we go to play, we lose each other
And then I start to cry for my mother.

So I find my friends and I have some fun.
I laugh as I eat my bun.
My friends and I laugh together
Because we will always stay friends forever.
As we go to play we shout
Hip hip hooray!

Shahad Hilmy (11)
St Cadoc's Primary School, Newton Mearns

Black

Black, black, black,
Black as black can be.
When it's close to Hallowe'en
Black cats I will see.

Black, black, black,
Black as black can be.
When the clocks go back
Blacker it will be.

Black, black, black,
Black as black can be.
Soon it will be summertime
So no more black I'll see!

Kayleigh Eddington (10)
St Mark's Primary School, Edinburgh

Autumn

Leaves are twirling in the wind
Leaves are swirling high in the sky
    Leaves are twirly
    Leaves are curly
    Leaves are crispy brown
    Leaves are twisty
The leaves are falling
. . . Down . . .
. . . On to the ground.

The wind is blowing to and fro
The trees are sighing high and low
The sun is shining high in the sky
    I think autumn's coming
    I think everybody has realised
The leaves are golden or even yellow
Orange or red.

Well that's autumn gone
And winter's nearly here.

Aimee Moore (10)
St Mark's Primary School, Edinburgh

Matilda

M any books she has read.
A bility? She has loads.
T hree was the age at which she could read.
I nteresting novels she has absorbed,
L oved 'Great Expectations'.
D ark-haired girl with big brown eyes.
A lways wants to read more.

Stuart Lockhart (9)
St Mark's Primary School, Edinburgh

Matilda

M atilda is her name
A nd a bright little girl she is.
T he amazing thing about her
I s that she can read lots of books.
L ovely and sweet she is.
D iscovering every day
A nd learning along the way.

Georgia Daisy Hill (9)
St Mark's Primary School, Edinburgh

Matilda

M atilda, you're the best!
A lways at the library.
T ell yourself you're very good.
I ntelligent.
L ovely.
D o know how to read.
A live!

Tiffany Wilson (9)
St Mark's Primary School, Edinburgh

Matilda

M agnificent
A ttractive
T alented
I ntelligent
L oveable
D aring
A ffectionate.

Amie McIntosh (9)
St Mark's Primary School, Edinburgh

Matilda

M y, oh my! What a great reader!
A t home she gets told off. At the library she has fun.
T oddling along using her brain.
I would never get near to reading a Dickens!
L ooking around the library for a Kipling.
'D addy, can I have a book?' she asks.
A ll day reading books; she does not get near the TV screen!

Stephen Pearson (9)
St Mark's Primary School, Edinburgh

Matilda

M agnificent girl.
A library lover.
T iny but smart.
I t's amazing what she knows.
L ovely to have her in the class.
D elightful people are Miss Honey and Matilda.
A n asset to her family.

Hannah Gibbons (8)
St Mark's Primary School, Edinburgh

Matilda

M agnificent.
A mazing at reading.
T ime to spare in the library. Yes!
I can't believe those parents.
L ittle but intelligent.
D efinitely amazing.
A terrific girl.

Nicolle Sims (9)
St Mark's Primary School, Edinburgh

Matilda

M inding her own business.
A smart and kind girl.
T all? Not quite!
I gnorant is she? Never!
L oving books all the time.
D ay and night reading away.
A lways caring and sharing.

Caitlin Mackay (9)
St Mark's Primary School, Edinburgh

Matilda

M agnificent.
A stonishing.
T aught herself to read.
I ntelligent.
L oony dad.
D ahl character.
A mazing.

Callum Costello (9)
St Mark's Primary School, Edinburgh

Matilda

M agic.
A mazing.
T alented.
I ntelligent.
L ibrary lover.
D ickens reader.
A polite girl.

Owen Duddy (9)
St Mark's Primary School, Edinburgh

Matilda

M agnificent as can be.
A mazing.
T errific at reading.
I think she's very smart.
L oves reading books by Dickens.
D oesn't like missing school.
A lovely girl.

Beth Coxon (8)
St Mark's Primary School, Edinburgh

Matilda

M agnificent.
A lways reading.
T oddles down to the library.
I ntelligent.
L ittle but smart.
D ad is rude.
A nnoying family.

John Harvey (8)
St Mark's Primary School, Edinburgh

Matilda

M agnificent.
A mazing.
T oddling to the library.
I ntelligent.
L ibrary lover.
D arling.
A dvanced.

Lucie Broadbent (8)
St Mark's Primary School, Edinburgh

On My Own

On my own I lay in my bed
Like a cow grazing in a field.

On my own I like to be stupid,
To be free like KJ and JB in
'Tenacious D the Pick of Destiny'.

On my own I like to laugh,
To jump and play.

On my own if I hear a horrible noise
I wrap my head in my pillow.

On my own I think of schemes
To make myself money.

On my own I blast my music.

On my own I draw a picture of the world
As I see it today.

And that's the way I do things.

Shaun MacFarlane (11)
St Mark's Primary School, Edinburgh

Matilda

M ad about books.
A very good reader.
T errific.
I ntelligent.
L ibrary lover.
D aughter of Mr & Mrs Wormwood.
A magnificent girl.

Aidan Haughey (9)
St Mark's Primary School, Edinburgh

On My Own

I go into my room and think,
I look out of my window,
What should I do today?
I know I should go on my PS2.

When I've had enough with it
I go outside and look for my friend,
But he is in his home.
I ask if he wants to come out,
We went on our bikes,
It was fun to play together,
We go too fast down the hill
And off ramps fast.
It is good fun.
When we are exhausted we go in,
Then we have our tea and drink,
Then go to bed to sleep for the next morning
And you say to your mum and dad,
'Goodnight!'

Stuart Cockin (11)
St Mark's Primary School, Edinburgh

Matilda

M atilda is mad . . .
A bout reading books.
T hey transport her . . .
I nto new worlds at the . . .
L ibrary. Her . . .
D ad prefers his lad instead of his . . .
A mazing daughter.

Jonathan Robertson (8)
St Mark's Primary School, Edinburgh

On My Own

On my own in my room
Doing things I like to do
Drawing pictures and writing stories
Being all alone is great fun that's right!

On my own on holiday
Dreaming of the things in the sea
Looking for fish and hunting for shells
Being all alone is great fun that's right!

On my own in the garden
Thinking of my friends and family
Watching all the birds go by
Being all alone is great fun that's right!

Now this is what I like to do all alone
On my own is great fun that's right!

Evie Kircos (11)
St Mark's Primary School, Edinburgh

Black

Black is the night sky when I'm asleep,
Black is everywhere,
Black hat with black suit,
Black socks with black boots,
Black is something you cannot always see,
Black is dark clouds with flashing thunder,
Black is ink in Victorian days,
Black is the spider that plays at night,
Black is a witch's hat and cloak,
Black is a witch's cat making you scream,
Black is everywhere.

Samuel Murray (10)
St Mark's Primary School, Edinburgh

On My Own

On my own, I like to sit,
Sit and think a little bit.
On my own, my fate in my hands,
I travel away to mysterious lands.

On my own, I like to lie,
Lie and read, for fun, that's why.
The author can take me somewhere else,
Instead of my bedroom in my house.

But all these adventures
Are inside my brain.
As I write them down
I'm travelling again . . .

Cameron Cunnea (10)
St Mark's Primary School, Edinburgh

On My Own

On my own I like to jump on my trampoline
To the sky in my sunny back garden.

On my own I like to go to my room
To sit and relax on my bed.

On my own I play in the park
And I swing on the swings.

On my own I like to read
All the books I can find.

On my own I like to play
On my bike as fast as I can.

And that is why I like to be on my own.

Kieran Davies (10)
St Mark's Primary School, Edinburgh

On My Own

When I'm on my own
I go in my room
And listen to music,
Or read a comic
With words like kaboom.
Sometimes I play football on my own,
Or go on my trampoline,
I also play my PS2
And computer too.
This is what I do
When I'm on my own
And to you it might not sound fun,
But it is,
Trust me!

Peter Connelly (11)
St Mark's Primary School, Edinburgh

On My Own

On my own in my room
I think to myself
What will I do today?
I think I am going out to play.

On my own in my room
I think to myself
A jog should do me good
So off I go around the park.

On my own in my room
I think to myself
I've done good today, I'm tired
So off I go to bed!

Naomi Baird (11)
St Mark's Primary School, Edinburgh

On My Own

On my own I like to play,
On my own I dream all day.
On my own I stay in my room,
On my own I am a tomb.

On my own I play football,
On my own I run up the hall.
On my own I bounce up and down,
On my own I never frown.

On my own I like to read,
On my own I don't fall to greed.
On my own I love to draw,
On my own life is just braw!

Nico Colarusso (10)
St Mark's Primary School, Edinburgh

On My Own

I don't like to be on my own
Because I sometimes groan.
I like to play my PSP but I'd
Rather have a Nintendo Wii.
It is nearly 2008 so I hope this year
Is going to be great.
I like to ride my bike.
I like to eat a healthy bun
It helps me run.
I don't when it is right to fly
My massive kite.
That is what I do on my own.
Yeah!

Sean Melville (11)
St Mark's Primary School, Edinburgh

On My Own

On my own I like to play the PlayStation
And search the Internet.

On my own I practise football
And golf in the garden.

On my own I collect cool stones
And watch telly.

On my own I play on my trampoline
And ride my bike.

On my own I like to run
And play in my room.

On my own I like to play tig
And climb big trees.

On my own I like to draw
And write very long stories.

It's great on my own,
It's just great!

Aidan Duddy (11)
St Mark's Primary School, Edinburgh

When I'm On My Own

When I am on my own
I feel relaxed and happy.
When I am on my own
I go up to my room
And listen to my mp3 player.
I sometimes watch a DVD,
I like it when I am on my own
Because I can read my books
But I often just fall asleep.
I like it on my own,
I must do it often.

Sinead Blyth (11)
St Mark's Primary School, Edinburgh

The Writer Of This Poem

(Based on 'The Writer of this Poem' by Roger McGough)

The writer of this poem
Is smaller than a mouse
As fit as an athlete
As bendy as elastic

As hot as a stove
As giggly as a laughing hyena
As funny as a monkey
As good as gold

As loud as a siren
As cool as a cucumber
As clever as a cat
As daft as a clown

The writer of this poem
Likes a bit of fun
You will probably find
Her running in the sun!

Chloe Hannant (10)
St Mark's Primary School, Edinburgh

Autumn

The nights are fair drawin' in
Days shorter and cooler
Swirlin' leaves through the air
And skies are no getting any bluer.

Windy nights, long cauld days
Red, green, broon or gold
And the leaves have braw colours
'Til they curl up and get 'auld.

Bairns go oot trick or treating
They get lots of sweeties
And they canny stop eating!

Emily Berri (10)
St Mark's Primary School, Edinburgh

Me, Myself And I

I like listening to my music,
Slouching on my bed.
I like drawing silly monsters,
With me, myself and I.

I like to think about tomorrow,
Sitting on my bed.
I like to think about the big blue sky,
With me, myself and I.

I like to be in my sitting room,
Watching some TV.
I like to be in my bedroom,
Sitting looking through my window.

I like to do all those things,
With, myself and I.

Erin Kennedy (10)
St Mark's Primary School, Edinburgh

On My Own

I like to draw
And I like to gnaw
On my favourite meal
I like to do anything I feel.

I like to jump and ride my bike
And do anything I like.

I like to write
And fly my kite
On a windy day
And that's what I like to do.
I am on my own tomorrow
So . . .
Hooray!

Daniel Kinghorn (11)
St Mark's Primary School, Edinburgh

On My Own

On my own in my room
I sit on my own and think,
I think about my animals, friends and family

On my own in my garden
I sit on a bench and think,
I think about the hills and all the things I've said

I like to think about people in wars,
Families getting torn apart,
How much better it would be if people could get along.

To take my mind off things I do sports like horse riding,
Every jump takes away a sad memory
And swimming flushes away my worries.

Louise Doyle (11)
St Mark's Primary School, Edinburgh

The Writer Of This Poem

(Based on 'The Writer of this Poem' by Roger McGough)

The writer of this poem
Is as good as gold
As bright as a light
As cool as my dad

As small as a mouse
As fast as a tiger
As sharp as a shark's teeth
As kind as my mum

As good as my family
As young as can be
As clean as a polo shirt
As clever as a dictionary

The writer of this poem
As handsome as the world
As hard as a rock
As cold as the wind.

Jacob Curran (10)
St Mark's Primary School, Edinburgh

The Writer Of This Poem

(Based on 'The Writer of this Poem' by Roger McGough)

The writer of this poem
Is as tall as a tree
As keen as a bright moon
As pretty as a princess.

As bold as a brick wall
As sharp as a pencil
As strong as a wrestler
As tricky as a bent nail.

As smooth as silk
As quick as a cheetah
As clean as a whistle
As clever as a computer

The writer of this poem
Is bad at rhyming so,
How she wrote
This poem no one
Will ever know.

Hollie Charleston (10)
St Mark's Primary School, Edinburgh

Autumn

Hidden beneath the red, yellow and golden leaves
A little hedgehog lies sleeping.
Around the chestnut tree
Conkers lie waiting for children to come.
Inside a soon bare tree,
A wise squirrel thinks of its hidden larder.
Before the clocks go back
Children play outside in the fading light.
Along the streets it's Hallowe'en,
Children are dressed up for their trick or treat.

Harry Dyer (9)
St Mary's Primary School, Greenock

Daydreams

My teacher thinks I'm reading but . . .
I'm abseiling in Lincolnshire,
Jumping down walls at really quick speed.
I'm playing bagpipes for the Queen on 'Britain's Got Talent'.
I'm a Ninja, throwing shurikens, kunais, fists and feet.
I'm flying through snow, white as sugar.
On a snowboard as well on the ski slope - going really fast.

My teacher thinks I'm listening but . . .
I'm actually free running at the annexe,
Vaulting, cat leaping and somersaulting.
I'm riding in a limo to Blackpool eating the best cuisine.
I'm boxing with Rocky Balboa, I have just left hooked him.
I'm surfing in the Algarve carving waves.
I'm sword fighting with Jack Sparrow.
I'm beating Rey Mysterio in a fight.
I'm running a marathon.

Jamie Millar (10)
St Mary's Primary School, Greenock

In The Dark

I see my wardrobe standing like a coffin.
My dressing gown looking like the Grim Reaper.
I start to sweat.
I see the TV and aerial looking like an alien
Or a monster getting hungry.

I hear the old ghosts going through my stuff.
Footsteps going upstairs.
Someone behind me breathing heavily.
Chains clanking as though someone is coming for me.
Howling from within the house.

I feel wild animal skins.
Covers holding me prisoner.
Water in my glass feels like blood.

I can't wait until it's morning again!

Matthew Skilling (10)
St Mary's Primary School, Greenock

Daydreams

My teacher thinks I'm reading . . .

But I'm actually on the QE2 in the jacuzzi eating chocolate-
dipped strawberries.
Two seconds later I'm playing number 25 in the old firm match
and I score,
Thanks to a setup from Jan Vennegoor of Hesselink!
Gordon Strachan goes crazy.
When I get into the dressing room I get sprayed with Lucozade
And then I get a limo home.

My teacher thinks I'm listening . . .
But I'm actually flying with the Red Arrows and doing stunts
And making loop-the-loops.
One second later I'm in Ireland playing on the trampolines with my
cousins and on the tractors.
I'm down in Dublin having a hot dog and having a nice cold drink
of Club Orange!

Daire Coyle (9)
St Mary's Primary School, Greenock

In The Dark

I see my globe sitting innocently like a loose head.
My wardrobe standing straight like a coffin.
My jacket lies like a man hung by the gallows.
The shadows on my wall lurking mysteriously.

I hear wind that's blowing like monsters breathing.
Wood creaking, are robbers invading my room?
Outside I hear dogs howling as if in pain.
Downstairs the TV's chanting away like aliens talking.
Outside I hear horrible screaming - a torturer?

I feel my cup of water at the side of my bed, it feels like blood.
The headboard of my bed is like bars in a jail.
The covers on my bed feel like ropes holding me down.

It's daytime soon but tonight . . . I'll be back for more!

Matthew Fulton (10)
St Mary's Primary School, Greenock

In The Dark

I see shadows on my walls, they look like wild animals.
I look at my teddies and it's like a stampede of rushing aliens
                                                          at my feet.
I look at my wardrobe and it's like a coffin, I am frightened Dracula
                                                          is inside.
Car lights shining through my window, is somebody searching
                                                          for me?
I look at my television, it looks like it's about to eat me!

I hear howling from the foxes in the cemetery.
I hear footsteps in the house, I think it is a robber.
I hear rustling trees outside and I have a shadow on my window,
                                                          is it a monster?
I hear doors creaking, my mum and dad are aliens.
My jewellery is clattering as if it's a ghost.

I feel like I'm caged when I'm in my bed.
I also feel my furry toys are skins of wild animals.
I feel my covers are like ropes holding me down.
My pillow is so soft it feels like I'm sinking.
I feel like when I'm in my bed I'm on a boat rocking in the middle
                                                          of the sea . . .

I can't wait until it's light!

Christy Forbes (9)
St Mary's Primary School, Greenock

Autumn

About an old pond lies a frog waiting for it to rain,
While above a rusty old gate sits a squirrel looking for its next bite,
Across the garden lies a worm waiting to be eaten by a hungry robin,
After the sun goes from the summer days, people are sad,
Against the window stands a woman fixing her hair,
While all along the sky, swallows say their last goodbye.

Nicole Bradley (10)
St Mary's Primary School, Greenock

In The Dark

I see my TV light - moving planets?
I think I'm in space looking out of a window.
My light dropping from my ceiling,
Is it going to hit me on my face?
The silhouettes of my books as if they are coming to get me.
I go to my bed and I start to hear knocking.
I think there are vampires floating by my window.
My sister's TV is on, she is watching Harry Potter.
I hear the spells, it sounds like Voldemort and Harry are fighting
                                       in my back garden.
My dad's putting cutlery away - clanking and rattling.
I think there's a robber in the house.
I feel books at the end of my bed.
Is it someone reaching to kidnap me?
I feel the sweat trickling down my neck,
I think it's blood.

Thankfully it's morning, I'm free - for just now!

Callum McDade (9)
St Mary's Primary School, Greenock

Autumn

In the autumn some animals' journeys end,
But in the spring new life begins once again.
Hedgehogs hibernate in their homes,
While leaves start to cover the garden gnomes.

Animals hibernate because when winter comes
There's no food except some meager crumbs.
Worms come out because the birds are away,
With the leaves boys and girls begin to play.

Squirrels crawl about the ground,
Leaves get blown round and round.
It gets a little colder every day,
Some boys and girls wish it were May.

Stephen Kane (11)
St Mary's Primary School, Greenock

Daydreams

My teacher thinks I'm reading . . .
But I'm being chased by 1,000 angry snapping turtles on-board
a boat.
I'm fighting a great white shark with a harpoon.
I stab it in the mouth and it sinks down.
I'm in a tunnel of sand running from a giant monster scorpion.
Its slimy black fangs wriggling hungrily around its face.
I'm on-board Admiral Nelson's ship blowing Napoleon's fleet
to pieces.
I'm on a safari watching tigers fight with bison.

My teacher thinks I'm listening . . .
But I'm in the Amazon fighting giant mosquitoes with an axe.
I'm fighting in a battle with a huge sword *clank, clank!*
I'm swimming with whales dodging their huge tails.
I'm flying high in a huge hot-air balloon.
I'm being attacked by a huge angry rhino.
I'm exploring mountains that touch the clouds taller than everything.
I'm exploring Canada, all the trees are huge and mighty.

Charlie McCartney (10)
St Mary's Primary School, Greenock

Autumn Time

Crunch, crunch, crunch go all the leaves,
They no longer help hold a home for bees.
The flowers all wither and start to die
And I wake up to a blue-grey sky.

The days are over in a blink
And at night the stars twinkle and wink.
It is a really pretty sight,
I want to look at them all night.

Children no longer play on the street,
But gather around the fire for heat.
My cat begins to lounge about,
Autumn's in and summer's out.

Lauren Robinson (10)
St Mary's Primary School, Greenock

All About Autumn

In the gardens the hedgehogs can't wait
Until the time approaches to hibernate.
Under the pond the fish and their mates
Swim around looking for some tasty bait.

All around the garden walls
I listen to the beautiful calls
Of the birds in early dawn
As I snuggle up in bed with a great big yawn.

I look at the park across the road,
I see the grass all scattered in gold.
The leaves have fallen from the trees,
Autumn has begun, everyone is pleased.

Under my feet I hear the leaves go crunch,
Now it's time for my mid-morning brunch.
Wholesome and tasty, the soup my gran makes,
As well as her mouth-watering cinnamon cakes.

I say goodbye to my animal friends,
It's awfully sad as autumn comes to an end.
But walking home I think to myself,
This is a season I would definitely recommend!

Charis Jackson (10)
St Mary's Primary School, Greenock

On Safari

O n safari you will see lots of animals
N o one can say you won't like it.

S ome of the animals will be friendly
A nd some will be your enemy!
F or the elephants
A nd the
R hino are totally different
 I would say you will need to choose for yourself.

Caryn Mearns (10)
St Mary's Primary School, Greenock

Autumn Ways

Trees rustle as squirrels are busy
Filling the inside of the tree with food.
People run over crushed leaves,
They all think autumn is good.

Oak trees are letting go of their conkers,
Falling to the ground, waiting to be found.
Migrating birds are flying to find their warmer homes.
Hedgehogs no longer wander the gardens,
It's time for them to go to sleep.

Patchy fog and shorter days,
All around the garden you see the wasps lay.
As I walk along my garden path I can see
Leaves scattered around my birdbath.

Some of the animals are asleep
And leaves are piled in an enormous heap.
Seasons are passing far too fast
And now autumn is nearly past.

Megan Clark (11)
St Mary's Primary School, Greenock

Colour In Autumn

The Earth is full of colour
And autumn is here once again.
The leaves are crimson and scarlet,
But lie out in the drizzling rain.

Crunching beneath my feet
Are the leaves golden and red,
Lying on the crispy ground
As if it's their cosy little bed.

The crispy coloured leaves
Have fallen off the big oak tree,
Leaving the branches bare,
I don't like that, but that's just me.

Rachael Robertson (11)
St Mary's Primary School, Greenock

Autumn

In the clouds as the last bird flies,
Some sleepy animals begin to shut their eyes.
In the garden behind the shed,
Some hedgehogs are gathering sticks for their bed.

In autumn behind the huts,
Some squirrels bury their hazel-brown nuts.
On Hallowe'en some kids are in for a scare,
Because the branches on trees are bare.

In autumn on the ground,
Some hedgehogs are purposely moving around.
That is all because spring has come,
Now all the birds hum and hum.

Gianluca Porceddu (11)
St Mary's Primary School, Greenock

Autumn

Under the big stone
ants are busy building a new town.
Summer was here but has now gone
and we are going to get autumn.
Inside my pond there are lots of fish,
sometimes completely covered by the fallen leaves.

Under the old oak tree lies crispy leaves
and a sleepy hedgehog.
Birds can no longer hide because
many of the leaves have fallen down.

Behind the garden shed
I hear some deer
eating the last of the autumn flower beds
while some birds fly away to the south.

Courtney Patton (10)
St Mary's Primary School, Greenock

Hallowe'en

Hallowe'en night
Gives me such a fright.
The eyebrows are raised
And the kids are praised.

Hallowe'en is very cold
And it's also very old.
People smoke
And kids tell a joke.

Cars go fast
As they go past.
We walk across the streets
As we ask for sweets.

Iona Gisbey (10)
St Mary's Primary School, Greenock

Autumn

Across the skies birds are flying to their new home
towards the sun.

by the pond frogs are hiding underneath some rocks
dreaming of rainy days to come.

Inside the fox's den the young cubs wait patiently
for food from their mum.

Below the chestnut tree conkers lie waiting
for children to find them to play.

Over the fence and through the reddy-gold leaves
a squirrel searches for food.

High up in a tree you can see a bird's nest,
no birds, only broken eggs.

Behind the stone wall there is a farm where woolly sheep
lie waiting for morning to come.

Aidan Watt (10)
St Mary's Primary School, Greenock

Autumn Days

Over the hedge and on top of the shed,
There sits a robin beside his bed.

The hedgehog looks up as the golden leaves are falling,
Then he turns round and the little birds are calling.

The sneaky squirrels scamper away
To find their home to sleep for the day.

I can smell hot soup that my mum is making
And my dad's fresh home baking.

Children are running around street corners,
Trying to collect all of the falling conkers.

When autumn is gone the animals will awake
And rummage through the bins for a tasty piece of cake.

Heather Ramsay (10)
St Mary's Primary School, Greenock

When The Autumn Comes

When the conkers fall out of the chestnut tree
My friends and I collect them for free,
We get some string and then we sling,
I will win the battle.

I like it when I hear the autumn leaves crunching
And squirrels munching on nuts
Or on little bulbs that gardeners have carefully planted.

Beside the garden pond there's a little frog hiding under a stone
Thinking of rain to come.
While high in the sky
Swallows fly to their new home.

A little hedgehog lies under its twiggy home
Waiting for spring to come.

Stephen Daisley (9)
St Mary's Primary School, Greenock

Autumn Time

Leaves are crunching beneath my feet,
They're flying around and not staying neat,
Conkers are waiting ready to be found,
The last of the leaves are falling to the ground.

Hedgehogs and squirrels are ready to sleep,
Gathering food that they must keep,
Hallowe'en is almost nearly here,
This is the children's favourite time of year.

Never forget the gunpowder plot,
Everyone loves fireworks, who does not?
Fireworks are hidden underneath the ground,
Ready to make a big, loud sound.

Children are getting on their scary masks,
Ready to scare the neighbours at last,
Candles are in pumpkins ready for tonight,
To give the kids a terrible fright.

Time to curl up in my warm house,
Wrapped up in blankets on the couch,
Sipping hot chocolate with sprinkles on top,
It's now too chilly to go out and shop.

Robyn Wilson (11)
St Mary's Primary School, Greenock

Boom!

They make colours as they fly
Shooting up into the sky.
They make noises in the night
Giving people a big fright.

The noises they make are very loud,
You can hear every sound.
As they go *boom* and *crash!*
You would think a window has smashed.

Boom and *crash* as little babies cry
And fireworks go into the sky.
People put on a big display,
'Look at that!' is what people say.

Ainsley Brennan
St Mary's Primary School, Greenock

Children In Autumn

A little girl walks along the lane,
She has on her coat because it's cold again.
She finds a conker beside the big oak,
When she passes the pond she can hear a toad croak.

She sees a squirrel gathering food,
Then sees it hiding it under some wood.
The little girl is putting on her Hallowe'en clothes,
A mask, a wig, a clown's red nose.

She knocks on doors saying trick or treat,
Hoping to get something tasty to eat.
Pumpkins lying at every door
And fake spiders scattered all over the floor.

The animals are starting to hibernate,
Winter is coming, I guess it's just fate.
The weather is going cold and bad,
Autumn is over, I guess I'm just sad.

Rebecca Keane (11)
St Mary's Primary School, Greenock

Hallowe'en RIP

On Hallowe'en night
Ghosts come out
To play with witches
And vampires.

When you go to a door
To trick or treat
A witch and vampire
Might come out
To eat you and
Your candy as well.

Connor McLeod (11)
St Mary's Primary School, Greenock

Autumn

The leaves are falling off the trees,
They're being blown around the cities,
As the wind carries them up and down
They land in gardens,
Some coloured a golden-brown.
Beyond the winter spring will come
And the leaves will grow on the trees again.

The last bird flies as autumn dawns,
Animals will sleep until spring comes,
Squirrels gather their food and then
They bury them under the ground so when
Winter arrives and there's no food near
They dig up the nuts they buried last year.

Hallowe'en is here, it's time for some fun,
Bonfire Night has begun.
I don't want autumn to end,
I can't wait until it comes again.

Siobhan R Riddoch (11)
St Mary's Primary School, Greenock

The Scary Haunted House

Once there was a scary haunted house
And it had a little tiny mouse.
It crept and squeaked all over the place,
You would think it could be in a race.
This mouse had a big horrible face indeed
It always liked to eat seaweed.

This big boy called Stephen
Went to put something in the bin,
He was brave enough to go in.
So he went up the hill
Just like Jack and Jill,
Then he arrived a little bit ill.

He crept in very scared and sad.
This adventure's he's doing is very bad.
'Argh!' Something was at his feet.
He thought it was just a sheet.
It was that mouse
Which always crept around the house.

Stephen went back home
And he was all alone.
He was playing on his phone
And never went back to that dreadful home.

Dominic Jack (10)
St Mary's Primary School, Greenock

On Safari

S lowly the lions move
A fter they have rested
F or many hours
A frica is quiet
R ising early
I ndeed they are.

Paul Dorrian (11)
St Mary's Primary School, Greenock

In The Dark

I see my teddies, their faces look like the faces of old prisoners.
My wardrobe looks like a door to another world with zombies that
                                                    live there.
The trees outside look like people trying to smash my window
                                        and come and catch me.
The shadows of the boxes in my room look like a monster from
                                                    another world.
My school uniform looks like somebody hanging by my bed.

I hear glasses, it sounds like a person robbing us.
The cutlery clashing – is somebody finding the sharpest knife in
                                        the house to kill me with?
The sounds of the wood contracting makes me think somebody is
                                        in the loft above my room.
I hear the wind whistling outside it as if a ghost is breathing hard.
I hear footsteps downstairs and it sounds as if someone is walking
                                                    about in my house.
Who could it be?

I feel my fluffy pillow at the bottom of my bed, it feels like a big, soft
                                                    cuddly bear is there.
I feel sweat at the back of my neck but I think it is blood.
I feel cold wind and it feels as if a ghost is passing by me.
I can't wait till it's morning!

Nina Hughes (10)
St Mary's Primary School, Greenock

My Little Sister

O livia is my little princess!
L ove her very much!
I love her to bits!
V ery cute with her little blue eyes!
I like the way that she smiles!
A ll babies are cute but the cutest is Olivia!

Lianna Marshall (10)
Slaemuir Primary School, Port Glasgow

Lots To Do!

I always have lots to do
Because the days are long
And I always plan ahead,
Like on Monday I could sing a song or even stay in bed!
On Tuesday I could ride a bike
And then go swimming or even visit Uncle Mike.
On Wednesday I could dance all day
Or keep it simple and just play,
Or I could stay in all day
And not even play!
On Thursday I could bake a cake
Or even eat a steak
And I might even visit a lake.
On Friday I could make a band
Or maybe play in the sand.
On Saturday I could watch birds
Or else just read a book.
On Sunday it is my time to relax
And get ready to play my day,
Just wait till Monday.

Shannon Archibald (10)
Slaemuir Primary School, Port Glasgow

Midnight Skies

Midnight skies are calming
When the summer nights go it keeps on coming back to us
And then it starts to snow.

Winter skies are cool and refreshing
When the autumn nights go it goes very quickly
But no one knows when.

The weather keeps on changing in the sky
But no one knows why.

Toni McCluskey (10)
Slaemuir Primary School, Port Glasgow

My Gran

My gran is a
Put your tootsies in my pocket,
A put your baby curls in my locket
Kind of gran.

My gran is a
Make it better with a treacle toffee,
A what you need is a nice cup of coffee
Kind of gran.

My gran is a
Money tree to me,
When I got stung by a bee
She was always there for me
Kind of gran.

Lucy Ballingall (10)
Slaemuir Primary School, Port Glasgow

Things I Like

I like to play on my PlayStation 2
I like Hallowe'en when I go trick or treating
I like to go out and play
I like to have a French omelette.

I like to watch Dr Who
I like to have beans on toast
I like my warm cosy bed
I like to watch DVDs on my laptop.

I like to get breakfast in bed
I like my Buzz game show
I like my Sing Star Rocks
I like to swim in a pool of magic beans.

Thomas McMath (10)
Slaemuir Primary School, Port Glasgow

Summer

Summer is my favourite time because we're all off school.
Running, jumping, swimming and splashing in the pool.
The weather's cool, so let's enjoy being off school.
Now is the time to enjoy summer while you can,
If you have a great time by yourself
When you go back to school say, 'I had fun by myself.'

Alistair McMath (10)
Slaemuir Primary School, Port Glasgow

Bonfire, Bonfire

Bonfire, bonfire, burn really high.
Bonfire, bonfire, light up the sky.
Bonfire, bonfire, come to me.
Bonfire, bonfire, don't ever die on me.

Josh Lochrie (10)
Slaemuir Primary School, Port Glasgow

The Day I Had

Oh Mum, oh Mum!
Look at that lady she looks like a nun.
Oh look at that lady she's trying to run
Or maybe she's trying to get that hot cross bun.

Then the day after that I went to the park
And found myself beside a big black shark.
I ran away to go and play
But then I blew away
And the wind was going sway, sway, sway.

Chloe Lowry (9)
Slaemuir Primary School, Port Glasgow

Chocolate

C hocolate is sweet, lemons are sour
H ot chocolate is good for cold winter hours
O h chocolate too good to share, oh
C hocolate ever so sweet
O h too
L ate my mum ate the last bit
A h chocolate back to the shop
T o buy more chocolate
E aten too much, going to be sick oh!

Christopher Coumparoules (10)
Slaemuir Primary School, Port Glasgow

That Moon

That moon up there in the winter sky
All spiked with stars on a frosty night
That silver moon shed a brilliant light.

Andrew McMath (11)
Slaemuir Primary School, Port Glasgow

Football

F un always
O rganised team
O uch
T ackles all the time
B all
A ttacking
L aughter
L ooking.

Lewis Macleod (10)
Slaemuir Primary School, Port Glasgow

My Friend Rebecca

Friends are good, friends are fun,
My friend Rebecca is number one.
I knew her for a long time,
All through my whole lifetime.
She moved in April.
She moved to England to Torquay.
It makes me sad to think about how kind she was to me.
She bought me sweets when she lived here
And she called for me every day,
But I'm sad now, so sad she moved away.

Hayley Williamson (10)
Slaemuir Primary School, Port Glasgow

Spooky

H allowe'en
A lways in autumn
L ots of sweets
L ots of leaves
O ld masks that scare people
W elly boots not worn yet
E ating candy all night long
E very day the leaves fall
N ow you will never put the lights out.

Fraser Tracey (10)
Slaemuir Primary School, Port Glasgow

Food

A tasty treat at any time,
Also fruit and vegetables are fine.
A hot cheese and tomato pizza
Is a favourite of mine.

Jack Attfield (9)
Slaemuir Primary School, Port Glasgow

Hallowe'en

H appy Hallowe'en
A nd people like to dress up differently.
L ike to scare people when they answer their door.
L ying to people that you have manners.
O wls flying to trees.
W olves barking as loud as they can.
E lves trying to steal candy.
E ven people don't like Hallowe'en but I know I like Hallowe'en!
N ot so nice! Vampires sucking people's blood.

Karla Coyle (10)
Slaemuir Primary School, Port Glasgow

Cockroach Sandwich

Cockroach sandwich
In my mouth
Hate the taste
But love the crunch
Cockroach sandwich
Munch! Munch!

Steven McCulloch (10)
Slaemuir Primary School, Port Glasgow

Autumn

A utumn
U nhappy about the dark
T rees bare
U ntidy gardens
M ist
N ipping at my nose.

Lee Marshall (10)
Slaemuir Primary School, Port Glasgow

Young Writers Information

We hope you have enjoyed reading this book - and that you will continue to enjoy it in the coming years.

If you like reading and writing poetry drop us a line, or give us a call, and we'll send you a free information pack.

Alternatively if you would like to order further copies of this book or any of our other titles, then please give us a call or log onto our website at www.youngwriters.co.uk

**Young Writers Information
Remus House
Coltsfoot Drive
Peterborough
PE2 9JX**

(01733) 890066